Vessel of Clay

The Inspirational Journey of Sister Carla

University of Scranton Press Series

PEACE, JUSTICE, HUMAN RIGHTS, AND FREEDOM IN LATIN AMERICA
In Honor of Archbishop Oscar Romero, Martyr and Prophet

Robert S. Pelton, C.S.C.
General Editor

Vessel of Clay
The Inspirational Journey of Sister Carla

By
Jacqueline Hansen Maggiore

with
Catherine McDermott Vint

Jackie Maggiore

UNIVERSITY OF SCRANTON PRESS
Scranton and London

Library of Congress Cataloging-in-Publication Data

Maggiore, Jacqueline Hansen, 1939-
    Vessel of clay / by Jacqueline Hansen Maggiore ; with
Catherine McDermott Vint.
        p. cm.
    Includes bibliographical references.
    ISBN 978-1-58966-217-9 (pbk.)
    1. Piette, Carla, 1939-1980. 2. Missionaries--Chile--Bi-
ography. 3. Missionaries--El Salvador--Biography. 4. Mis-
sionaries--United States--Biography. 5. Maryknoll Sisters-
-Biography. I. Vint, Catherine McDermott. II. Title.
    BV2853.C6P546 2010
    266'.2092--dc22

    2010005573

Permission for the use on pg. 47 of the verse of Victor Jara's poem,
Estadio Chile, granted by Joan Jara.

Distribution:
UNIVERSITY OF SCRANTON PRESS
Chicago Distribution Center
11030 S. Langley
Chicago, IL 60628

PRINTED IN THE UNITED STATES OF AMERICA

We dolly along in this crazy circus of life where so often the Divine Circus Master doesn't clue us into the act for tomorrow yet always gives us the strength to perform.

Carla Piette, MM
August 22, 1980
El Salvador

Dedication

CARLA HAS ALWAYS BEEN a presence in my life, carried closely in my heart. Her life is known, if known at all, because of her death in El Salvador just months before the murders of Maura Clarke, Jean Donovan, Dorothy Kazel, and Carla's mission partner, Ita Ford. Carla had answered Archbishop Romero's call "to accompany his suffering people." She came with an open heart and a brave spirit shaped by her years of mission work in Chile.

I have gained a deeper appreciation of Carla's strengths and weaknesses, her profound spirituality and underlying insecurities. She battled depression throughout her life, yet she found the strength to give of herself with energy, empathy, and life-enhancing humor. I've come to appreciate the words of Carolyn Lehmann, a former Maryknoll sister: "Those who didn't know these women—Ita and Carla—have a tendency to make them into some sort of saints 'out of this world.' But they were real, gorgeous, loving women, dedicated to the poor, and with all their own foibles, like any one of the rest of us."

During the 1970s, missioners in Chile led the way to proclaim a preferential option for the poor. *Vessel of Clay* is dedicated to all the real, down-to-earth, loving women who, like Carla, courageously served the poor in Chile and El Salvador during those terrifying times.

Contents

*MSA: Maryknoll Sisters Archives

CHAPTER ONE

Appleton and Milwaukee

WHEN CAROL ANN (CARLA) PIETTE entered Maryknoll's motherhouse at Ossining, New York, in 1958, she walked beneath the main archway inscribed with the words of Mother Mary Joseph, the foundress of the congregation, describing a Maryknoll sister: "I would have her distinguished by Christ-like charity and the saving grace of a sense of humor." For those of us who knew Carla, this description fits her to a tee. One sister, smiling at her memories, described Carla as "deeply contemplative... and crazy as all get out."[1]

Carol and I grew up together in Appleton, Wisconsin. In the 1940s and 1950s, Appleton, home of Lawrence University and the Institute of Paper Chemistry, was a thriving, middle-class community. We children saw very little poverty and almost no cultural diversity.

Carol Ann, the baby of the Piette family, was born September 29, 1939, in Appleton. Her brothers, James and Eugene, were fifteen and twelve; her sister, Betty, was ten. Rose Piette was forty-one when Carol was born and it is likely that she did not anticipate having a baby so late in life. Carol grew up feeling that she was a disappointment to her mother; she carried the heartache of that belief all her life. From her early years, Carol turned often to Betty, a kind, warm-hearted listener, for comfort and support.

Carol's mother was a homemaker whose life centered on home, family, and church. She prided herself on keeping an immaculate house. Carol's father, Jim, owned Piette Family Grocery; he was a respected business leader and an

1

outgoing man active in the community. He organized and served as president of the local United Grocers Association and was an officer of the National Retailer-Owned Grocers Association.

Carol found loving affection with her father; they were very close pals. Known as Daddy's girl, little Carol often rode with him in the truck to their grocery store on Appleton's main street. In earlier days, the Piettes had lived in an apartment over the store, but by the time Carol was born, her father had built the family an attractive two-story brick house. A formal family photo shows young Carol sitting on her mother's lap. Her brothers, so much older, are already young adults. Her sister, a teenager then, bears a close resemblance to Carol.

Carol and I first met in kindergarten. We shared an excellent grade-school education at St. Mary's with the Sinsinawa Dominicans and then went on to Appleton High School. Life in grade school was quite routine—the same twenty-nine students were together from first through ninth grades. Our days included daily Mass, May crownings, and prayers for the conversion of Russia. Classrooms competed with enthusiastic fervor to raise pennies to "save pagan babies," our earliest introduction to foreign missions. In our narrow, secure world, the only rivalry we knew was between parishes—our Irish St. Mary's and the German parish of St. Joseph's a few blocks away. Our biggest fears were the threat of Communism, the atom bomb, and polio.

In 1948, when Carol was in third grade, her father died suddenly at home after a massive heart attack. He was fifty-one and had not been previously ill. A close family friend later said that her father's death "seemed to have a very serious effect on Carol. She worshipped her father." The pain of losing her father was made much worse by her mother's refusal to let Carol see his body or attend his funeral. Mrs. Piette, like many at that time, believed that seeing a dead person would be harmful to a young child. Being kept away, however, only deepened Carol's grief.

For Carol, life at home became very different without

her dad. He had been a loving, calming presence and a window to the outside world. Now her mother, in her own grief and loneliness, seemed more distant and unable to comfort Carol. Mrs. Piette attended daily Mass and spent many long hours in the parish church in private prayer. Carol's brother Eugene, who had recently returned from Army service, enrolled at Lawrence University in order to live at home and assist his newly widowed mother. Carol's oldest brother, Jim, a Purdue University graduate, was already established in his engineering career in Ontario, Canada. Betty was studying nursing and lived miles away from Appleton.

In May 1950 Betty graduated from nursing school at Mercy Hospital in Oshkosh, Wisconsin. She decided to join the Air Force nurses and at once felt the sting of her mother's disapproval. "That's no place for a woman," Mrs. Piette objected. "What kind of women do that?"[2] When Betty met her future husband, Jack Frazier, in the service, her mother viewed his occupation with great disdain. Jack came from a professional circus family and had studied with the nationally renowned clown Emmett Kelly.

In spite of her mother's strong disapproval, Betty and Jack married at St. Mary's on May 17, 1952. Carol was bridesmaid. After their stints in the Air Force, Betty and Jack resumed their careers—she as a nurse and he as Corky the Clown, performing with small family circuses. They raised their family first in Michigan and then in Florida. Many times Betty visited home without Jack, because her mother continued to look down on him and treat him poorly.

Young Carol found Jack a breath of fresh air. He was fun, open-minded, easy to talk with—like a big brother. He taught her juggling and other tricks. Throughout her life, Carol was attracted to the clown persona. She easily amused her classmates—and, later, her fellow missioners—with her clowning, joking, and good-natured nicknames. Yet the clowning often concealed her sadness and self-doubt.

Any out-of-the-ordinary excitement in our grade school class usually revolved around Carol; she was zany, creative, at times irreverent, and full of bubbling enthusiasm. To our glee, she could quickly sketch on the blackboard a cartoon of Sister Placid, the principal, while Sister was out of the room and then hastily erase it before Sister returned. She once led several of us in some juvenile silliness that got us kicked out of eighth-grade choir, much to the frustration of the inexperienced and extremely nervous young sister in charge. Nobody's parents were pleased. Carol's mother, very upset and disappointed, chided Carol, "I hope some-day you'll be a sister whose students misbehave so terribly." Carol just laughed about that unlikely prospect.

Despite her fondness for foolery, Carol could be strong-willed, blunt, and direct. She was always willing to question authority, challenging especially anyone who acted self-important or hypocritical. I can still see the dumbfounded expression of a young assistant priest who found himself stymied by her question: "If you've taken a vow of poverty, how can you be driving that big, fancy new car and go on ski vacations?"

Carol's willingness to question authority did not extend to disobeying the rules at home. One childhood friend re-members that at the height of the polio epidemic—when swimming pools and movie theaters were off-limits or closed and we children were warned not to assemble in crowds—her parents allowed her to go bike riding with Car-ol because Carol could be trusted to obey the rules.

Although obedient, Carol was willing to resist her moth-er's wishes when matters she cared about deeply were at stake. Carol had never seen much need for material things for herself and considered clothes especially unimportant. When her mother wanted her to have new shoes for our ninth-grade graduation picture because her old ones were torn at the seams, Carol laughed and said, "What's wrong with these?" The formal photograph, taken in church in front of the communion rail, shows Carol in the front row, wearing her favorite old shoes.

When we were in high school, the rules set by Mrs. Piette and Eugene were unusually strict. Carol was not allowed to join her friends in the usual fun of high school—ballgames, pep rallies, sleepovers, dating, and dances. Again, although she might challenge authority in other settings, she seemed obedient and accepting of the limits at home. We classmates did not see her rebel or even hear her complain.

As she matured in adolescence, Carol at times felt criticized by her mother for being too tall, too heavy, and too awkward. She was big-boned and, at five feet eight inches she towered over her mother, a lovely petite lady with silver hair and flashing brown eyes. Carol often covered her pain at the perceived criticism by laughing it off and by making fun of her own looks. She drew even closer to Betty, also tall and somewhat heavy and with a large, generous heart.

She enjoyed giving nicknames to others, a talent she exercised throughout her life. To her I was simply "Hansen," my family name. Our good friend Karen Crowe became forever Crowbar. She adored hilarious comics, including Louis Nye on the Steve Allen Show with his famous "Hi-Ho, Steverino!" Her own favorite saying became "You've got to take the bitter with the sweet."

Unlike most of us at Appleton High, Carol took both college prep and business courses and reached out to make friends in both groups. She pushed us college-bound students not to feel so superior to our commercial classmates. She served as officer in both the French and Commercial Clubs. She had a special love for French studies, became enamored with all things *francaise*, and often decorated her notes with the fleur-de-lis.

Just as Carol's spirit and heart were large enough to unite the sides of a traditional high-school divide, her character was large and complex enough in another way to encompass an unusual blend of frivolity and seriousness. As Karen (Crowbar) recalled, "The silly, the unusual, the unexpected always amused her. She was also more serious than the rest of us—a sort of crusader in her thoughts. Yet, she encouraged me to pursue the ordinary mundane interests—hair, boys, fashions, Elvis, etc."

During high school Carol had babysitting jobs and a part-time job at a downtown shop. It may have been at the shop that she was groped by someone she trusted, likely an older worker, perhaps her boss. She was stunned and uncomfortable but did not share the details with friends. We only knew that it was a frightening and chilling experience for her.

Her favorite job was at the Lawrence University Library. She greatly admired the head librarian, Hastings Brubaker, a distinguished scholar and teacher and a collector of art objects, which he lent to the library for public displays. University students dedicated the 1960 yearbook to him as a statement of their admiration. For Carol, he was a hero—sophisticated, cultured, urbane—whom she could admire from afar. She joked often—and we often teased her—about her fondness for Mr. Brubaker.

In the fall of 1957 Carol and I headed together to Marquette University in Milwaukee. On our very first day in the big city she led me to her two favorite places—first the downtown Cathedral of St. John the Evangelist for a visit and prayer and then to the fairgrounds for fun on the midway and carnival rides. It surprised me that she knew where to go and that she chose the cathedral. It was no surprise that she would head for the carnival.

In dorm life, with lots of chat time, I grew to know Carol more deeply. Her prayerfulness and devotion to her deceased father amazed me. His presence was real to her, kept alive in her mind and prayers. For all her life, as her fellow Maryknoll missioners would later know, she relied only on Daddy to wake her each day—he was her personal alarm clock that never failed. She was also devoted to St. Joseph, another father figure. She bubbled with enthusiasm about her intellectual, urbane heroes—Victor Hugo, Alistair Cooke, Pierre Mendes-France—as if she knew them personally. Her eyes sparkled as she talked excitedly about how glorious heaven would be! Why? Because it would mean being able to converse with Victor Hugo and all those other wonderful men.

At Marquette Carol developed a special admiration for the Jesuits as intellectuals—particularly her professors of theology, philosophy, and history, and the Sodality advisor. All the Jebbies (as we students liked to call the Jesuits) then lived in Johnston Hall, a campus building which also included university offices. For a short time, Carol worked at the Johnston Hall switchboard, which was close to the residence area, so she had even more chances to meet and chat with the Jesuits. A door leading to the residence was clearly marked Cloister and she joked many times about walking through that door as a prank: Would the area really be defiled by a woman's presence?

Sr. Catherine Verbeten, OP, a cousin of Carol's mother, said that even in grade school Carol had spoken to her about an interest in religious life. We childhood friends, however, knew nothing about it. At the back of Gesu, Marquette's campus church, Carol picked up a small brochure on vocations written by George Ganss, SJ. She quickly took its guidelines to heart and Fr. Ganss, a distinguished professor of classics and Ignatian studies, became her regular spiritual advisor.

Carol's family, like many Catholic families, was familiar with Maryknoll missioners through a subscription to Maryknoll Magazine. The Maryknoll Society of mission priests and brothers had been established in 1911 as the official Catholic Foreign Mission Society of America. One year later Mary Josephine (Mollie) Rogers founded the Maryknoll Sisters. A graduate of Smith College, she had seen her Protestant fellow students volunteer for international mission work and regretted there was no such opportunity for Catholic women. As Mother Mary Joseph, she became the first leader of the Maryknoll Sisters.

Carla's personal introduction to Maryknoll came in March 1958 when our sodality mission program featured Maryknoll sisters. Maria del Rey Danforth, MM, a journalist before joining Maryknoll, had recently authored *Her Name Is Mercy*, an award-winning biography of Sr. Mercy (Elizabeth Hirschboeck), a medical missionary who had worked in Korea. Mercy was a Milwaukee native and graduate of Marquette Medical School. At the sodality meeting, Maria del Rey spoke of her own mission experience, which included three years spent in a Japanese internment camp in the Philippines during World War II.

More than 150 students attended the program. Although I was duly impressed by the energy, humor, and adventuresome spirit of the Maryknollers, they didn't speak to my life—I heard no call. But Carol certainly did. She was profoundly moved and came away totally on fire. These women matched what she was looking for: purpose, depth, adventure, solid focus. And that was it. She continued regular sessions with Fr. Ganss. She agonized about going so far from her family, especially her mother. After much prayer and discernment, her decision to enter Maryknoll was firm.

Carol's younger cousin Mary Jo Thies has a vivid memory of the day Carol visited her home to tell Mary Jo's mother—Carol's father's sister—about her decision: "Carol was sitting in a chair close to my mom and when she told her, Carol had a radiant look on her face that can only be described as complete contentment and trust in God."[3]

In June Carol visited Maryknoll's Valley Park community in St. Louis for a personal interview. She emphasized to friends that she had to be sure of her motives, that her decision had to be a positive choice and not an attempt to run from problems, family, or the world. That summer, in preparation, she had dental work done and ordered new eyeglasses. She joked that her mother thought the fancy frames "might make a lady out of me." Her medical checkup showed a chronic bronchial ailment, which later was severely exacerbated by Chile's cold, damp winters.

Carol had expected opposition from some of her family, especially to her entering a religious order that would take her so far away from home. She was right about her mother's reaction: Mrs. Piette was sad, angry, and sometimes bitter. She spent her own life close to home and she thought that her youngest daughter's duty was to stay close as well. Throughout that summer her mother often broke into tears trying to convince Carol not to go. It was a painful time for both. Once her decision was made, however, Carol never wavered.

On July 24, 1958, Carol wrote to Lillian Bozak, our good friend from Marquette at home in Connecticut for the summer, "I've been ACCEPTED! I wish you all were here to share my joy with moi. I really feel so happy and gay that if convent life could add one more spark of happiness, I'd be simply out of this world." The next week Fr. Ganss came to Appleton to celebrate over dinner with her family. Carol was thrilled and exuberant about his visit: "It was all so nice and unrestrained," she wrote. "My mere liked him a lot!"

In early August Carol and her mother traveled to Mary-knoll, perhaps in an attempt to allay Mrs. Piette's concerns. Yet after the visit Mrs. Piette still tried to dissuade Carol from going. When she met my mother at church, she said that she hoped the strict atmosphere of the convent would prompt Carol to leave.

At summer's end, before I returned to Marquette, Crow-bar and I held a small going-away party for Carol. The honoree came dressed as Zorro, her new crusading hero, in a sweeping black cape and eye mask. My gift to her was a Bible. I later wondered if it was the Bible she treasured and clutched so closely throughout her mission life.

Carol was an avid smoker, the only one in our college group. She enjoyed having a cigarette, and perhaps a cock-tail, with my mom and dad that summer. When gearing up to leave for Maryknoll, she faced one more major decision: Should she quit smoking completely now? Phase down slow-ly? Or smoke as much as possible until she went through the convent doors? She chose the third option, of course, going all out, full steam ahead, as she would do so often through-out her life.

Crowbar saw Carol off at the Appleton train station, where she boarded to ride alone to Chicago and then to Os-sining, New York. Between trains, Carol sent postcards from Chicago to thank her. "Hope I didn't make you cry—don't worry—I prayed all the way to Oshkosh—Gotta take the Bitter to get the Sweet." She planned to see Lillian between trains at Grand Central Station, figuring that if her train was on time she could get to 8:30 Mass at St. Agnes Church (which she probably knew about because Bishop Fulton Sheen's televised sermons were broadcast from there) and still meet Lillian "under the big flag" at 9:30.

Carol entered the doors of Maryknoll on September 2, 1958.

CHAPTER TWO

Maryknoll, New York

IN 1958 MARYKNOLL'S RECRUITMENT was at a high point. Carol was one of the sixty-two postulants who donned the standard postulant habit of black dress, black veil, and white collar and cuffs that year. Maryknoll's postulancy was a nine-month period that preceded formal admission to the congregation. The women sometimes compared it to the nine months of pregnancy, a preparation for giving birth to a new self.

Although Maryknoll was more progressive and less restrictive than many religious communities, the rules for postulants—no talking, no mixing with novices, no special friendships, no twosomes—still necessitated a painful adjustment. Many young postulants were lonely: As Ita Ford wrote of her own postulancy a few years later, "It's lonely, not in the sense of being alone in a crowd, but in an emotional way. No one knows you well enough to be able to say the right thing when you need it."[1] Many had a hard time with the rules. All mail was censored, and public penances and public recitation of minor "faults" were routine.[2] By the end of Carol's first six months, about half of the women who entered with her were gone. Some chose to leave, some were asked to leave. These departures were never explained to the women who remained, so they were troubled by many unanswered questions and unsaid good-byes. Pat Cobb McKenny, a former Maryknoller, described the process: "A small piece of yellow paper would go on the bulletin board, with a notice for that individual to see the Novice Mistress," and that individual would be gone.[3]

Carol had a hard time controlling her laughter in the convent's strict environment. In September she wrote to Lillian, asking for prayers for self-control: "I have the duty of reading at breakfast. So far I've been able to suppress my giggles—however, for the rest of the day they flow rather freely—even in chapel, I'm ashamed to announce. When the priest in his homily spoke, 'for the test of the heart is trouble, and it always comes with the years,' naturally, I just about arose and started reciting the Cremation of Sam Mc-Gee!" She squeezed words in the tiniest handwriting on the tiniest piece of notepaper—and at the end, below her signature, was a teeny, tiny, barely visible Z, the secret mark of Zorro.

On June 24, 1959, the feast of St. John the Baptist, Carol received the religious habit of the Maryknoll novice—a dark grey wool habit with a white veil. She also received her religious name of Rose Carol. Each woman could submit three preferences for her new name. Sometimes choices included the postulant's birth name, since in many mission countries that name was required on official papers. I have always assumed that Carol selected Rose Carol partly to honor her mother, Rose. She may have also chosen it for the symbolism: She saw the rose as beautiful, delicate, perishable, but with thorns that made it painful to hold. In order to get to the beauty of the rose, you had to experience the thorns, the "bitter with the sweet." After she became Rose Carol, she delighted in signing her name with a drawing of a rose.

Carol survived the two-year novitiate, but not without some disappointments. Although she took religious studies, including a heavy emphasis on scripture and liturgy, she was not sent to finish college, as she had hoped. Her days were split between studies and work assignments; she worked in what she sometimes called the salt mines, doing routine kitchen and office work. On June 24, 1961, she took her first vows, received the simple silver ring engraved with the Chi Ro, the Greek symbol for Christ, and replaced her white veil with black. The novice mistress in her Pre-Professional Opinion described Carol as "friendly, outgoing, jovial, big-hearted, and generous, but rather naïve and tactless."[4] It sounds accurate. Carol Marie McDonald, MM, a friend in those novitiate years, recalled Carol as being in good spirits, very funny, and often egged on by others for their enjoyment.[5]

Later that summer Carol met Karen Peterlin, who came to Ossining after entering Maryknoll in Valley Park in 1958. Karen and Carol became very good friends over the next three years. Karen remembered Carol as very bright, but "what shone out in her was her soul which was so powerful." According to Karen (and emphasized by many who knew her), Carol had a special ability to connect closely with others and to listen deeply with an open heart. Karen also noted Carol's gentleness, describing her gestures: "She had a unique way of using her hands, turning them over as she spoke, ending with her palms up and stretched out to you."

Carol often gave little gifts of herself—drawings, poems, flowers, and even prized possessions. She held on to nothing. Said Karen, "She always pulled something out of her pockets for you—a stone, a flower, an apple, a seashell, a feather—but mostly she gave of herself. She was there for anyone. She often thought of herself as being a poor vessel for this work—but she was not a whiner or looking for pity. Instead she seemed to accept herself with her failings and saw the humor of it."[6]

Carol remembered that turquoise was my favorite color, so her notes to me were often in turquoise ink, accompanied by holy cards of a turquoise-framed Madonna. She embellished gifts of her poems with sketches and designs.

On one occasion, poems that another young sister had written were found in a locker inspection and the sister was ordered to read them aloud to the whole assembly. She was devastated at the prospect of revealing her private thoughts. She confided in Carol because she knew that Carol also wrote poetry. Carol listened with empathy and then suggested that she herself would volunteer to read as well, but that they would read each other's poems. Then no one would know whose voice was speaking. The sister was amazed, relieved, and comforted by the plan.

Carol could be similarly creative when she violated the rules. Foundress Mother Mary Joseph, an exuberant and compassionate woman, had said, "I obey the rules, but sometimes it's necessary to lay them aside." Carol, too, sometimes laid them aside, especially if obeying them caused someone else pain or if ignoring them could help someone. One example was her often being late for curfew at St. Teresa's residence because she was visiting the elderly sisters who lived in another building—reading to them, writing letters for them, listening to their stories. Since the door at St. Teresa's was locked after curfew and ringing the bell would get one in trouble, Carol devised a signaling system. She stashed a pile of acorns ahead of time so that when she was late she could throw them at the window of a sister whose room was on the second floor in the rear of the building. The sympathetic sister then let her in. But Carol would later feel guilty and confess publicly at Chapter of Faults.[7]

Visits from family were limited to once a month. With Carol's family far away—in Wisconsin, Michigan, and Georgia—their visits were infrequent. Her brother Eugene, who lived in Pennsylvania for a time, visited at least twice—in 1964 and again when Carol was at Maryknoll on furlough in 1976. From 1958 to 1964 her mother visited at least five times. After the 1964 visit, Carol wrote to Lillian, "My mother was here in May and although our visit was relatively hectic, it was the best I've ever had in that it was the truest. She saw me as a person, unique and different from her, and she can't quite accept this. The fact, however, that I am an individual with different values and reactions from her, is a revelation, and until we both face these things, our relationship will never improve. It's kind of hard for her, though, so if you have the memory, I would appreciate a prayer for her—Merci!" Lillian and her family, who lived in Connecticut, were more frequent visitors, at least during Christmas and summer vacations.

In early September 1961, after our own college graduation, Crowbar and I traveled together from Wisconsin (on a cheap redeye flight) to visit Carol. She was so excited that she sent a note: "I'm sure we'll have a great visit—even taking the bitter with the sweet. How I'd love to give you a memento of it: art work—ghastly; poetry—trite; essays—boring; trinkets or souvenirs—relatively hard to come by these days. 'But do good...to even nasty men and wicked city women' and pray for those who give you a dirty deal. There's where we are united—all striving for the ideal of Charity and for me—for us—to know we strive together, no matter what the distance that separates us."

Carol was mindful of her own faults and frailties; she saw herself as a weak and flawed instrument. She often expressed empathy for sinners and the need to reach out to them, emphasizing that the biggest sinners needed acceptance and communion rather than excommunication. In 1964 the sisters visited the World's Fair in Queens. The fair's theme was "Peace through Understanding" and its symbol was the Unisphere, a gigantic twelve-story replica of earth. The Vatican had a pavilion and Pope Paul VI visited the fair. Major American companies, including General Electric, sponsored pavilions to salute the space age and the expanding global horizon. Carol remarked that if even GE could be so inclusive of all mankind, why couldn't the church as community?[8]

***

By 1964 many changes were stirring in the world, the Catholic Church, and Maryknoll. Fidel Castro was in power in Cuba, and many feared the spread of Communism. Civil rights demonstrations in the United States culminated with the March on Washington in August 1963. The U.S. government's establishment of the Peace Corps was soon followed by the Catholic Church's emphasis on Latin American missions, the Papal Volunteers (PAVLA). President John Kennedy was assassinated in November 1963. In Chile, social reforms were underway following the 1964 presidential election of Christian Democrat Eduardo Frei.

The Second Vatican Council (Vatican II), called by Pope John XXIII, met from 1962 to 1965 and opened the way for far-reaching reforms within the Catholic Church. The synod's call for renewal included a strong emphasis on the participation of the laity, changes in liturgy, and respect for human rights and cultural differences.

At Maryknoll a general chapter meeting was held from July 5 to August 18, 1964. The sisters discussed the reforms of Vatican II and reaffirmed their mission identity. But there remained tensions and disagreements about the directions of reform. Many found the reforms—a stronger role for the laity, the elimination of the Latin Mass and Friday abstinence, the possibility of changes in religious habit—liberating. Others, like many Catholics worldwide, were uncomfortable with the changes.

At a departure ceremony on August 9, 1964, on the Maryknoll grounds, friends and family gathered to see each sister receive her mission crucifix and official mission assignment. Our college friend Lillian was there, as was the family of Ann Teasdale, a young girl whom Carol had tutored for first communion.

Carol was ecstatic to receive a mission assignment to Chile. To her old friend Crowbar she wrote, "Look what Our Father has given to me. ...I'm thrilled but sort of full of awe and aware of the tremendous trust I must have." She thanked Lillian's family for all their visits, prayers, and gifts and wrote of her upcoming departure: "Then the beginning of the already growing process of becoming more of Christ for the church and my new people is in process. Please pray for us all: we're so human in many good ways—but more than these ways will be needed for the growth of the Church in Latin America." She was eager to be doing, to be active for others. And perhaps she was also eager to leave the unending community discussions regarding the impact of Vatican II.

Yet moving on to Chile, as exciting as it was, meant leaving two dear friends. Carol's friendship with Karen Peterlin had been critically sustaining during her novitiate years. And with Lillian Bozak, who had visited often and was now studying for her doctorate in theology at Marquette University, she had enjoyed discussing theology, liturgy, and the impact of Vatican II.

That summer, before leaving for mission, Carol visited home. On August 30 the Appleton Post-Crescent ran an article about her under the headline "Nun Will Cope with Poverty, Communism at Chile Mission." Carol described her upcoming journey on a fruit boat, "Just the bananas and us!" Language school in Pucón would last a year, the newspaper said: "Contact with the Chilean people will be minimal; however, light conversation with area children will enable the new nuns of the mission to try out their Spanish." While home Carol also enjoyed an exhilarating ride—dressed in full habit, of course—in the flashy red sports car of Crowbar's brother.

Karen Peterlin vividly recalled driving Carol from Ossining to the Grace Lines ship in the Red Hook area of Brooklyn. "We got hopelessly lost in this sea of warehouses. I stopped to ask a longshoreman where the Grace Lines were and he said, with a very thick Brooklyn accent, 'It's on foist and toidy tord. Sistah, you make a u toin right here.' He stopped traffic to repeat the directions 'Foist and toidy tord.' I had never heard this strong accent before and started to laugh but tried not to offend this helpful man. Carol, sitting next to me, was laughing harder than I. Several cars now waited for me, and the longshoreman started gesturing wildly and repeating, 'u toin, sistah, u toin.' Finally I snapped out of my laughter, turned the car around, waved thanks to the guy and headed toward First and Thirty-Third. Our ribs hurt from laughing!"[9]

Carol, along with Helen Carpenter, MM, and Chilean Sr. Ondina, MM, left Brooklyn at 9 a.m. on September 19, 1964, for their three-week voyage on a banana freighter to Chile.

Helen remembered that Carol liked to stay out on the deck at night to pray under the stars. Always eager for adventure, Carol also tried to remain on deck when the ship was within a hundred miles of a hurricane and severely buffeted by the storm. The crew quickly put an end to that adventure.[10]

Their journey took the sisters through the Panama Canal. At stops in Panama, Ecuador, and Lima, Peru, they spent the day touring with sisters who worked in each country. Carol was depressed by her first exposure to poverty, particularly by the extremes: the homes of the wealthy situated next door to a shabby, run-down shack for the maid. She wrote to her sister, Betty, "Lord, I believe, help my unbelief." (Mark 9:23-24).

CHAPTER THREE

Pucón, Chillán, and Buzeta

MARYKNOLL SISTERS HAD BEEN a significant presence in Chile since 1950, when they were invited by the Chilean hierarchy and by Maryknoll priests, who had worked there since 1943, to found parish schools for the poor. The first to arrive was Marie Estelle Coupe. On October 9, 1964, Sr. Rose Carol Piette, soon to be known as Hermana Carla, became the fifty-fifth.

Upon arrival in Chile, Carla, impatient and forceful, immediately began to assert her own preferences. First, she entertained the sisters at their welcome party with a hilarious skit, a takeoff on a Bill Cosby comedy routine of "Moses and the Ark." Next, she insisted on changes in their customary prayer ritual, replacing the rosary with a scripture reflection. The stunned sisters went along with the reflection that first night but soon changed back.[1] Carla had pushed too soon.

Carla first stayed in Pucón, a tiny town five hundred miles south of Santiago. Nestled between the pristine Lake Villarrica and a smoking volcano, Pucón was surrounded by spectacular scenery. Most Pucón residents lived in extreme poverty. The five-star Hotel Antumalal, however, catered to rich tourists on skiing and mountain climbing vacations.

The sisters' small house was close to the lake, with a view of the active volcano and the mountain range separating Chile from Argentina. During Carla's early years in Chile the rule of silence was still observed in the house and

19

conversation was allowed only during a designated time after dinner. "Imagine being silent during an earthquake," said a sister who was there during an unusually powerful one in 1960.[2]

Language training in Pucón was a program of total immersion for the length of a school year. Carla, in addition to pursuing language studies, eagerly reached out to families living nearby. She visited neighbors, invited them to join the sisters' scripture reflections, and pitched in wherever she was needed. She soon learned to give injections for the caretaker who suffered with cancer, and his wife came at all hours of the night to summon her when he was in pain. Carla became very close to the family, praying with them every day, and was greatly saddened by the man's death.

Her experiences in Pucón introduced Carla to the reality of the lives of the poor—to their sufferings and deprivations and also to their strengths and generosity. At Christmas 1964 Carla wrote to the Lauderts, her Aunt Katherine and Uncle Arn, "To study the language right now is my mission. But even in studying, I see a great deal when I open my eyes. There is great poverty, lack of clothes, food, and housing that we take for granted. But I believe more that real poverty consists in the lack of hope that can push a man to despair. This I ask now, please, to pray for, and to practice with me in filling up in the Whole Church what is lacking here."

Carla often wrote poetry about her experiences and reflections on the most difficult Bible readings. As she continued to struggle with her own weakness, she wrote, "We come pretty close to sinking—but we never do. Ah yes, we all try, but He knows how often we fail."

During vacation time, January to March, the language students moved from Pucón so that working mission sisters could stay there to relax. On that break, Carla was sent to a Maryknoll convent in Temuco, a couple of hours away, where she met Pat Cobb, MM. Temuco, too, had stunning views, of five active volcanoes and the snow-covered mountain range—the *cordillera*. The sisters lived in the poorer section of town where corrugated tin roofs covered shanties with cardboard walls. Here Carla enjoyed being of service and living closer to the poor.

Almost from the beginning, Carla found the pace of language studies—her year of "light conversation with area children"—far too slow. Impatient to learn, she began studying the famed Chilean poets Pablo Neruda and Gabriela Mistral, not the easiest reads in a new language but fascinating and meaningful to her.

Not only the slow pace of learning bothered her at Pucón: The damp and dreary weather aggravated her chronic bronchial problems and lowered her spirits. During the rainy season—eighty-five days of wintry rain and cold—it was impossible to keep warm. Temperatures outside were in the low forties and inside the sisters' house there was no central heat. Only one room was warmed, by a kerosene or wood stove.

Carla soon pushed so hard to move on that Stephanie Marie Kazmierczyk, MM, her superior in Chile and previously the principal of San Vicente School in Chillán, called Mary Ellen Manz, MM, now principal there: "Will you take her? Maybe you could break her in and she could do something in the school." Mary Ellen agreed, expecting Carla to arrive in a week or so. To her surprise, just a day later she found Carla smiling on her doorstep in a teeming rainstorm. "Hello! Here I am!" Carla announced, clasping the one little suitcase she had brought on the long bus ride from Pucón. Mary Ellen described Carla as a nonconformist who was often critical of the status quo but also extremely sensitive and able to connect deeply with people, especially the poor and outcasts.

She was perhaps the only person who got herself out of language school early. She made her own way, compelled to move on, to get started, to be involved.

Chillán, a city of 50,000, is 250 miles south of Santiago, halfway between Pucón and Santiago. The San Vicente parish and school, begun by the Maryknoll Sisters in the 1950s, served seven hundred children of poor peasant families. Pastor Tom Golden, MM, had come to Chile in 1952. Richard Brooker, MM, who later became pastor and a good friend of Carla's, had arrived in 1963.[3] Carla's friend Pat Cobb was already teaching there. In addition to Mary Ellen Manz (whom Carla nicknamed Microphone Manz for her loud voice) and Pat, the sisters included at various times Joan Ratermann, Ceci Santos, Becky Quinn, Nancy Casey, Theresa Brown, and Louise Gillen.

San Vicente's church, school, and rectory faced the plaza. A long wooden building, flanked by two outhouses—one for boys and one for girls—housed the primary grades. Two ancient olive trees provided shade and yielded a fine crop of olives each year. On the other side of the building were rows of fig trees, "which the boys would pick easily by climbing out of the classroom windows during recess and stuffing their pockets," said Pat.[4]

In 1939 an earthquake had devastated Chillán and killed nearly 30,000 people. The new cathedral was built to be earthquake-proof and was dedicated to the victims of that quake. Also, in the Chillán area in 1954, two Maryknoll priests had died in separate rectory fires.[5] Thus, the sisters' convent, a two-story pink stucco building, was built with safety and strength in mind. Much lovelier and sturdier than other buildings in the area, it had a roomy living room that was used mainly for larger meetings. In addition to a dining room and a fairly modern kitchen, there was a more casual community room—the only room with a direct heat source. The stove burned sawdust, which "gave off a delightful heat, an even dry warmth which could take your mind off the pervasive, bone-chilling cold which lurked right beyond the door," said Pat.[6] Upstairs were several tiny individual bedrooms. Off the kitchen was a comfortable bedroom and bath for a young Chilean girl hired to do the cooking and laundry. A chapel, located just off the living room, was painted a spinach green identical to the color used in the church. The sisters called it the Green Icebox because of its total lack of heat; in winter it was icy cold.

Although a newcomer, Carla did not hesitate to assert

herself. Upon meeting a distinguished bishop, who addressed her with the familiar *tu*, Carla answered him in the same familiar manner. Her superior, Mary Ellen, was horrified. The bishop corrected her, saying, "My dear Sister Carla, you do not use *tu* with me, your bishop." Carla simply smiled and replied, "But why not? Are you not my Father? And do not children address their Father in this way?" He was indeed persuaded and they became friends.

Very early in her stay Carla announced plans to visit the newspaper editor to protest the lack of coverage relevant to the poor. Mary Ellen stopped her with a reminder that she was brand new in the community and shouldn't be so quick to judge. "So don't do anything like that for a year," said Mary Ellen, assuming Carla would forget about it. Exactly a year later—much to Mary Ellen's surprise—Carla told her that she was off to make the visit. The next morning the paper featured the work of the Maryknoll sisters with a picture of Carla and Pat Cobb, along with a letter of appreciation from the editor referring to Carla as the *amable madrecita* (lovable little mother) from the United.States. She had won another friend.

Carla, who had no teacher training, initially taught second grade. Many of her students were nine or even older and still had great difficulty with reading. She enjoyed teaching and gradually developed her own unorthodox, self-taught techniques to reach those who had the most trouble. She was especially drawn to the slowest learners, whom she affectionately called her "cement heads."

Recent research had shown the value of a new method of teaching reading by crawling: The cross-lateral movement stimulates brain development and memory. Carla, inspired by a workshop she attended, created a special program at San Vicente to work for an entire year with children of all ages who struggled with reading. None had crawled as babies. The floors in their homes were often just mud, dusty or damp, depending on the season. Leaving a child on the floor could invite pneumonia. There was also danger from the braseros—open fires in metal containers very low to the ground that were used for cooking and to dry laundry. So Carla crawled with her pupils to stimulate the motor part of their brains. She was dedicated to this training technique and wrote to me, "We crawled together and read together and eventually made some slow progress." I was amazed that she, so far away in Chile, was even aware of this newest research in brain development.

In July 1966 she rhapsodized to Aunt Katherine about her students: "Naturally I think the 42 little ones I have are the best in the whole world—they are very poor yet have the rich spring of joy common to all children. They help me in my weak moments in Spanish and still have a beautiful spirit of optimism, not dampened by the bitter facts of life for the poor here."

The teaching sisters were not limited to the classroom. In her letter to her aunt, Carla described home visits to her students' families and the "simple but at times desperate needs of our people for shoes, books, clothes, and sometimes food." She thanked her relatives for sending a donation to help with these basic needs.

Not all of the students lived near the school. Many lived in the mountains or the outlying countryside and some stayed in the city with relatives during the school week. A small donation from St. Mary's, our home parish in Appleton, enabled Carla to purchase a bicycle, which made some home visits a bit easier.

Tom McDermott, MM, pastor in Galvarino, the earliest school of the Maryknoll sisters in Chile, said of them: "The sisters won the hearts of the people, and the parents that I could never reach were reached. The sisters were not just in a classroom; they were in the homes and they disciplined both the child and the parent. They were pastors."[7]

Ceci Santos, MM, a tiny woman whom Carla nicknamed Holy One or Little One, lived with Carla in Chillán for six years. She recalled that Carla always reached out to those most in need. She told the story of Mariano, a fourteen-year-old boy Carla first saw polishing shoes on street corners. She often stopped to talk with him and they became friends. Concerned because he had never been in school, Carla persuaded him to enter her class and also tutored him after school. He learned so well that he was promoted to Ceci's fourth-grade class, where he was much older and taller than the others but an eager learner and the best-behaved student. Later Mariano found a job in another town but always came to visit Carla when he returned to Chillán. In 1973 he visited her in Santiago and in late 1979 they met by accident in Chillán when she was saying her good-byes before leaving Chile.

Ceci, along with several other Maryknoll sisters who knew Carla in those early days, had vivid memories of Carla's statements about dying: "If I'm still alive at 40, please beat me to death! I don't want to be a grouchy old menopause lady!"[8] She told many friends that she hoped to die as poor as can be, meaning naked as she came into the world, without possessions. She prayed that by the time she died her heart of stone would become a heart of flesh. She pushed herself constantly toward greater charity and to rid herself of comforts and possessions.

With so many women of different personalities and differing opinions sharing close quarters, conflicts were inevitable. Carla clashed strongly with several women, especially those with equally forceful personalities. The sisters from Chillán remember Carla having periods of depression, during which she was low-spirited and withdrawn. They attribute these to her chronic bronchial problems exacerbated by the cold, her sensitivity to the sufferings of the poor, and her history of family heartache. Carla seemed to believe that no one in her immediate family, except for Betty and Jack, understood or supported her choice of vocation.

During her years in Chillán she wrote hundreds of poems that reflect her journey: deep sadness at the poverty and powerlessness of the pueblo, joy in nature, and prayerful searching. In "Prayer of the Marshmallow," written in August 1966, she wrote: "I'm poor—teach me to be dependent./I'm soft—help me to withstand bruises./I cling to all that touch me./Take away the fear that makes me shake,/and give my jello heart/a peace as real as you are." In "Poverty," she spoke of herself as holding back: "When will I shed my finely woven answers/and stand before Him poor, bare, dirty?"

The Maryknoll sisters were active in many schools and missions throughout Chile and often visited each other and gathered at regional meetings. Even those who never lived with Carla remember the clever, entertaining skits she improvised. Her gift for clowning and spontaneous humor included a special talent for mimicry and exaggerating the funny mannerisms of everyone, including the Superior and the guests.

One sister laughingly described her own experience when she made an official site visit as a member of the Maryknoll governing board. She loved Carla's sense of humor and recalled her as a "profound and simple" woman. Her visit came after relaxation of the rules governing the sisters' religious habit, and she felt quite pleased with herself for choosing a handsome modern suit and wearing no veil. She was stunned and in gales of laughter when Carla came forward to greet her dressed in the old-style religious habit and veil and then knelt on the ground to kiss her ring with a great flourish. Later that night Carla, still dressed in full habit, entertained the assembled sisters.[9]

Carla's clown persona, however, hid much sadness. "People only saw the 'clown' in her, while inside she was bleeding," said Joan Muriel Higgins, MM. Carla felt so deeply with the people, especially the poor and outcasts, that often she was dragged way down by their sorrows as well as by her own.

***

In Chillán Carla was blessed to find new friends in Maryknoll sisters Becky Quinn and Pat Cobb. Becky had been in Chile since 1955 and taught in Chillán from 1961 to 1967. Eight years older than Carla, she was a warm, nurturing woman, who perhaps reminded Carla of her sister, Betty.

Carla and Becky shared a similar heartache: When Becky, an only child, first joined Maryknoll her parents, like Mrs. Piette, had hoped she would return to them soon.

Pat and Carla first met in Temuco, where Pat had taught since 1959 and which Carla visited on breaks from Pucón. The two women shared artistic talents and a delightfully quirky sense of humor. Pat, nicknamed Sport by Carla, had fond memories of those years and of Carla's antics. When Pat was seriously ill, bedridden with mono and typhoid, Carla volunteered to care for her when others declined. Carla's approach to healing the spirit was unique: "One day to cheer me up, she brought a nanny goat to my room that one of the parishioners had given us. This one was so very dainty. She tiptoed around almost as if she were a child, wearing high heels. And these visits continued for weeks. Carla was insatiable when it came to enjoying life!"

Pat recalled that on one occasion the pastor saw her and Carla leaving the local brothel. He scolded them, aghast at the impropriety. "It was our custom to visit the home of each student at least once, and we knew that several of the mothers of our kids worked at the brothel. For a poor woman with no other skills it was about the only line of work they could do, and it allowed them to feed their children. The women were delighted that we had gone to see them, and we all had tea and scones together. The madam, in fact, was a pillar of the Church. Later, when the pastor lodged a complaint about our having gone there, Carla was more than ready to point out the value and intrinsic dignity of these women, and suggested that he make a pastoral visit, too. Of course, under the circumstances, it was far easier for us to do so than for a priest to visit the local madam."

Another time when Pat and Carla were making home visits, the sweet aroma of fresh bread coming from a bakery they passed tempted them and they promptly bought hunks of the hearty bread to munch as they walked along the road. This was unusual behavior for nuns, and Dr. Roberto Mattatal, a local doctor and church supporter, driving home for *onces* (afternoon tea) with his family stopped his car when he saw them. He chided them for eating on the street when they could be eating with his family. The sisters accepted his ride and spent a delightful afternoon with his family of seven children. The Mattatals warmly embraced the two sisters, welcoming them into their family as Tia Carla and Tia Patricia.

Later, when Pat needed a surgical procedure, Dr. Mattatal performed it for free with two provisos: that she adopt one of the puppies in their dog's new litter and that his young son, Gonzalez, be allowed to visit the dog. So the dog Samba become Pat's pet and Gonzalez visited weekly.

Pat, the person closest to Carla in those years, perhaps understood Carla's depressive moods better than anyone. She acknowledged that Carla's periods of depression were very real, often worsened by her bronchial difficulties in the cold climate. However, depression did not keep her from working: "Carla was very complex, yet amazingly simple in her trust in Jesus Christ. When she was in the doldrums, it only served to draw her closer to Him....She would throw herself into parish activities, meetings with the teachers, and parents, and each evening, when she really didn't have a shred left, she would be in the chapel...giving the ups and downs of the day all back to Him. Her depressions served to get her to know Christ on very personal terms."[10]

Several sisters remembered Carla's spiritual depth and the insight shown in her scripture reflections. Each morning the sisters took turns leading meditations in the Green Icebox. Pat and others looked forward to Carla's reflections because "she could put such a fresh spin on the Gospel—it was food for her soul."

Joan Ratermann, who lived and taught with Carla for several years in Chillán, noted Carla's consuming love of the poor and her capacity to feel the sufferings of others as if they were her own. Joan's strongest memory is of Carla's great love of the Scriptures. "To pray with her was a wonderful experience! She saw in the Scriptures, because of her openness to the spirit, things that I did not see."[11]

Many colleagues chuckled to recall Carla's program of "father formation," her informal but persistent efforts to educate the missionary priests (whom she nicknamed the Daddy-Os). She prodded them toward a stronger pastoral commitment to justice for the poor. She emphasized that many of them were too removed from the poor and that they erred by trying to transplant traditional North American parish structures to Chile instead of adapting to the needs of the culture.

Ray Hill, MM, who served as Regional Superior in Chile, recalled, "The Sisters were always ahead of the priests in their thinking on where the Church should be going...The work they were doing was outstanding, really working with the poorest of the poor. Something we committed ourselves to but didn't do. And they were doing it."[12]

In Chillán Carla worked closely with Richard Brooker, MM, a quiet, reserved man whom she affectionately named Babbling Brooker. When I visited Fr. Brooker at Maryknoll in 2005, he immediately asked me, his eyes twinkling, "Do you know what she called me?" He delighted in the name.

***

The later 1960s brought continuing change and turmoil, both within Maryknoll and beyond. Our country witnessed the assassinations of Malcolm X, Martin Luther King, and Robert Kennedy, the riots that erupted at the 1968 Democratic Convention in Chicago, and the long ordeal of, and the protests against, the Vietnam War.

In 1968 the assembly of Latin American bishops, held in Medellín, Colombia, strongly supported liberation theology. The Medellín assembly became known as the turning point in the Latin American church's commitment to a "preferential option for the poor." Brazilian archbishop Dom Helder Camara, a strong advocate of justice for the poor, led the way.

Vatican II had opened the door to changes within the institutional Catholic Church, and several years after the council ended, there were still major differences and ten-

sions within each religious house on subjects ranging from
social justice to religious habits and liturgy. In obedience to
the mandate of Vatican II that all religious orders reexam-
ine their purpose and charism, the Maryknoll Sisters held
a special chapter meeting in Ossining in 1968. The discussion was so difficult that there were fears the congregation
would break in two. It was truly an identity crisis. In the
end, the sisters reemphasized their mission identity of action based on faith. Latin American attendees, who already
worked closely with the poor, were strong advocates for liberation theology.

As in other religious communities, the change in religious garb was also an issue. For some, changes came too
fast; for others, not fast enough. In 1968 the Maryknoll Sisters issued a brochure showing options of dress; it stated,
"Our changing style of dress is merely one way to adapt to a
fast-changing world." The Maryknoll Sisters never banned
the original religious habit but instead offered choices to
their members: traditional garb, modified garb, or contemporary dress. The only requirement was that all sisters
wear the simple silver ring inscribed with the Chi Ro. By
1973 most sisters wore contemporary clothing. In 1970 the
Maryknoll Sisters also changed their governance structure,
moving from leadership by a mother general to the election of a president and a central governing board. Their first
president, Barbara Hendricks, MM, served eight years and
established a collegial model of participatory leadership
based on consensus.

Vatican II's strong emphasis on the role of the laity
created new possibilities for lay missioners. Many priests
and religious women began to question their vocations and
many left. Worldwide, the Maryknoll Sisters lost almost a
third of their professed members between 1966 and 1974, a
drop from 1,430 to 993.[13]

Watching friends leave the congregation brought heartache to those who stayed. For some, the pain was akin to
the pain of a divorce. In addition to keenly missing those
who left, those who remained inevitably had to rethink their

vocations. Carla and Pat supported each other during this difficult period of questioning and self-doubt.

Carla was scheduled to take her final vows in 1967. In October 1966 she wrote about her struggle to Mother Mary Coleman (on stationery she decorated with Charlie Brown drawings): "My heart is so full of searchings. I look for the road God points out but it's so foggy sometimes and, being so weak, I know my glasses aren't even well cleaned. This last year before vows has been so hard. But I do ask each day to die, vowed to Him, in this life. I'm trying to be what He wants me to be but it's so hard. So day by day I guess He leads us."

During 1967 seventeen sisters from the Chile region left the Maryknolls; several of them were from Chillán. This loss "was devastating to us, and caused great suffering," said Joan Ratermann, who was then in Chillán.[14] The departures were a shock and difficult adjustment for the entire parish community. Because it had suffered so many losses, the parish chose to celebrate Carla's positive commitment by inviting everyone—teachers, parents, and children from the school—to attend the ceremony.

Carla made sure that her final vows, on June 24, 1967, were meaningful for everyone who was present. Much to the priest's surprise, she did not face him and the altar, as was the custom. Instead she interrupted him and walked to the podium to speak her vows in Spanish directly to the people: "Because I love God and Maryknoll and you, my dear, dear friends, I am able without wavering to promise to live as a Maryknoll Sister and to serve you until the day I die." Her superior, Mary Ellen, viewed Carla's surprising pronouncement as an unusual and beautiful way to say "I am giving myself to you people, to the Chilean people." Everyone was touched.

To her Aunt Katherine Carla wrote:

> Chillán's winters are cold so I'm sure I was the only MK Sister making her commitment to Christ in a winter coat and a scarf wrapped around my neck.

[Carla borrowed these from the mission barrel.] Many of my people were there—parents of my little ones, fellow teachers, and people I knew from home visiting. And afterward they all came and gave the big Chilean abrazo. For many I'm sure the whole idea of vows to an unseen God was a completely new idea. Since it was in Spanish that I said the words just before communion, I think it affected some people. Our vocation will always be a mystery and without a deep faith and trust in God it could never be, so I can understand why it's not the simplest thing to grasp. But the most important thing is that we live what our Christ teaches, and vows aren't for that. So we all end up trying together, no?

By 1969 Carla was teaching sixth-grade math and science. She enrolled in summer studies in education at the Universidad de Chile and in October 1971 was proud to receive a certificate as Profesora de Educación Primaria.

In the summer of 1969, she visited home on furlough, as was customary in Maryknoll after five years in mission. She took courses in religion and Old Testament at Edgewood College in Madison, Wisconsin. Her mother hosted a small reception and fundraiser for her at their family home. Helping Mrs. Piette was Mrs. Ed (Dorothy) Frahm, whose daughter Joan, our classmate from St. Mary's, was now Sr. Michaeleen of the Agnesian nursing order. When Carla returned to Chile she sent a thank you gift, a special Chilean candle, to Mrs. Frahm. She gave it to her daughter, who treasured the gift and lit it very rarely. Years later, Michaeleen shivered to recall that the candle burned out on August 23, 1980, the night that Carla died.[15]

Carla's Christmas card in 1969 illustrated her admiration for the generous hearts of the children of the poor. The drawing is of a little Chilean boy bringing gifts to Baby Jesus: "Here I bring You some pears—even tho they aren't ripe, they're good when they're cooked." She explained, "These words show the spirit of the children here. When

I asked a little boy what the Magi brought to Jesus, he answered, 'a blanket, a pillow and some shoes.' These are the necessities he saw and responded to. And such is the mission we have here now."

Chile's cold, damp winters continued to be hard on Carla. She called Chillán "this dark valley of tears" because of its heavy, seemingly endless winter rains. Her Christmas card of 1970 mentioned fighting a bad case of pneumonia, a chronic affliction not helped by the cold and damp and by the absence of central heat.

In 1964 Eduardo Frei of the Christian Democrat Party had been elected president of Chile on a reform platform, and his administration achieved significant agrarian reforms. However, Chile's main source of wealth, the copper industry, continued to benefit mainly U.S. companies. The level of poverty, especially among landless peasants, increased. The moderate political party splintered.

Salvador Allende, the candidate of the Popular Unity coalition party, won the presidency in 1970. He was the first democratically elected Marxist president in the hemisphere. Political opponents, covertly assisted by the United States, had spent millions to prevent his election and inauguration. After he took office they continued to foment political turmoil and economic disruption. To destabilize the Chilean economy the U.S. government cut off its loans and sources of credit and led a campaign for a boycott by international creditors, including the World Bank. Economic sanctions were intentionally designed to produce a drastic shortage of goods and rampant inflation, and to inflame rebellion against Allende.[16] By the summer of 1971 Carla's letters mentioned shortages of food and that most men were out of work and in low spirits.

Allende acted quickly to improve the lives of the poor. He nationalized copper mining and other major industries (angering U.S. corporations who lost control), increased workers' wages, and strengthened land reform. Both the socialist government and the Catholic Church considered land redistribution as fundamental for the dignity and rights of rural campesinos. Programs included health, nutrition, and housing projects, such as the development of *poblaciones*[17] around major cities. The Allende years, said Maryknoll priest Dick Sammon, were a time of "a popular government and a wonderful experience for the poor."[18]

Allende's efforts benefited the poor but drew strong opposition from the powerful vested interests. Within Maryknoll, as within Chile itself, sharp political division and tensions developed during these years. The covert opposition forces, Chilean capitalists, and the U.S. government portrayed Allende as a dangerous Communist. Some Chileans, however, believed that Allende was a leader who could bring about a healthy melding of Christianity and socialism. In 1971 eighty priests who worked with the poor formed Christians for Socialism; the group grew to include several hundred members—Catholic priests, brothers, and sisters; lay persons; and Protestant pastors.[19]

Among the Maryknoll missioners in Chile, there was no political consensus; their concern was simply to decide who could best serve the poor. Carla stayed away from political statements at this time and declined to sign a petition circulated by Charlie Curry, MM: "I couldn't agree with all they were accusing the U.S. of, so I didn't sign their two-page masterpiece," she wrote Pat, then home on furlough. The petition, which was sent to President Nixon in July 1971, defended Chile's election of Allende and called on the United States to support elected leaders and not to interfere with Chilean sovereignty. Many Maryknollers were among the seventy-nine signers.[20]

That same year a new program of catechetical preparation began at San Vicente. No longer would children prepare for first communion by attending classes taught by the nuns. Instead, the sisters would work with mothers and the mothers would then teach their children. Carla visited families to encourage their participation. At first the mothers felt incapable, thinking that religious instruction was the job of the sisters and priests. But Carla patiently explained, "This is the age of the laity and really no one knows Christ perfectly but we're all on the same road." Small groups met each week to discuss the meaning of Bible stories. The groups came together a few times a year for a participatory para-liturgy and to socialize, sometimes playing charades inspired by Bible stories. Carla mentioned in a report to Maryknoll that initially it was difficult to persuade husbands to allow their wives to participate. Later, when she went to say good-bye to each family before she left Chillán, the husbands begged her to stay. They had seen their wives and children benefit. "So it kind of said a lot for personal contact and real trust in the Spirit working," she wrote.

Of course, not every group meeting was perfect. In a letter to Pat, Carla described a less than satisfactory one: "Just returned from my terrific meeting in the población with Brooker...It was the most *unified* meeting ever—*none* showed! Not a one! So Brooker and I came back after I visited every home. It was just like the gospel—everyone had an excuse. Soooo...I never promised you a rose garden."

***

In addition to the political upheavals and economic disruptions in Chile in the early 1970s, Carla also suffered more personal disruption and loss. Her friend Becky Quinn moved out of Chillán to a new assignment. Her friend Pat Cobb had been questioning her own vocation for several years.[21] In 1966 Pat had visited home on furlough to be with her sister Joan, who was newly widowed and had ten young children. Pat struggled with whether she should remain to help Joan but eventually, still feeling torn, returned to Chile.

When Pat went to Maryknoll on her next furlough, in May 1971, she remained troubled by her sister's situation. Although the other Maryknollers in Chile expected Pat to return, Carla knew that she was considering leaving the congregation. The pain of keeping this secret, the possibility of losing Pat, and the fact that Pat agonized for months without making a final decision all weighed Carla down. Letters flew frequently between the two women that summer and fall, with Carla nudging, guiding, and finally shoving

Pat to seek guidance. Carla, whose own answer to difficulty was to pray more and seek help from an advisor, repeatedly pushed Pat to find an advisor, make a retreat, get some help. "It's not healthy to stay in the middle of the road," she wrote, "since from either way you can get *squashed*."

Pat and Carla had supported each other through the difficult years of doubt and questioning when so many others left Maryknoll and Carla decided to stay. Now, although Carla supported Pat, she knew that Pat's final decision might permanently separate them. To sustain and nourish herself, Carla turned to prayer. When all went wrong she headed for the Green Icebox: "I just flop down and say Lord, what am I, mean Carla, doing here...Lord, do you hear me, Lord... and the Lord says, calm down and just rest yourself. I say to the Lord—He's all I got, so He gives me a push and says, Go ahead, I'll take care of the 'Sport....I believe He will."

Carla, who had leaned on Pat for so long and shared so much with her, missed her deeply. In August, she wrote that she came home from Mass in tears, thinking of Pat's decision, fearing that she would not return. "I want you to be happy, Pat, I really do. Yet I know I'll miss you terribly. Please tell me soon." Carla mentioned that she was brushing Samba, Pat's dog: "Why all the sudden care for her? She's all I have left."

Carla also included a reflection on her own experience of Christ:

> Christ to me is a man, strong and gentle, who has let himself be known thru four amateur writers called evangelists. What other man, so secure in what he has believed and lived, would let himself be revealed thru two fishermen, a tax collector and a witch doctor? Anyway, that's how we met—Christ and I. As we came to know one another—I thru reading, thinking, asking, knocking, crying and questioning, I saw He was more than just strong. He had the values I want. He saw people sick and said, "your sins are forgiven" and then healed them. He saw the innards of people

and didn't care about the exterior. He saw hypocrites and didn't shut up but told them they were whitened sepulchers and yet he saw big blokes who were with him for years and didn't know him and He just said— "You will!" when the Spirit comes.

Christ to me is this man who has all the answers this mixed-up world is looking for and that's why I want in my small way to let others know Him. I see people who have his qualities—His straightforwardness and gentleness in Mary Ellen, His compassion and understanding in Jaime, His love of beauty and depth for friendship in you. But each one has just a part. No one really has all but Him and to me He is real and my only star of hope. Also I hear him say, "You didn't choose me—I chose you" and to me that means a lot. I'm not studded with goodness. He knows I'm mean and shekel loving. But in it all, His love, which is a mystery that words won't grab onto, helps me to keep going.

Our love has meant a lot to me in the past seven years. However, if that love would die, Christ to me doesn't die. He still loves me and I in my own poor way can still say in my heart, "I love you, Christ—help me." Seeing Christ in others is important cause we're human and only thru other people can He give us the assurance we need.

Later that fall, anticipating that Pat would decide to leave, Carla wrote, "Only Samba has been told you'll never be back. All we want is your peace of mind and heart." She promised to send a trunk of Pat's clothes. She did not apologize for pressuring Pat to make a retreat, urging this "not to change your decision but to give Him a chance to speak and lead you now."

Pat was formally granted a six-month leave of absence from Maryknoll in December 1971. That February Carla wrote, "I'm so happy you'll make the rendezvous with the

Lord." Pat made her retreat and, at the end of her leave, of-
ficially withdrew from Maryknoll. Two years later she married a widower with children. Perhaps she had been questioning a call to a marriage vocation for some time. Perhaps
it was too difficult for her to share this clearly with Carla.
Perhaps it was too difficult for Carla to hear.

Carla's grief at losing Pat was twofold: She lost a close
friend and Maryknoll lost another sister. Her sadness brought
her to a turning point, another moving on. Throughout her
life in Maryknoll Carla often displayed restlessness and a
desire to move out of the larger convent structure and closer to the poor. In February 1972, the time of hearing that
Pat was finally making a retreat, Carla suddenly announced
that she would leave Chillán and move to the Buzeta mission in Santiago. She had recently visited the parish of San
Juan de Dios in Buzeta, where Helen Carpenter, her com-
panion from the banana boat, and Carol Marie McDonald, a friend from the novitiate, worked. Perhaps staying in
one place for seven years was enough for her. She talked of
wanting a "heart of stone," possibly to avoid the pain and
heartache of loss.

Carla announced her leave-taking suddenly, without ex-
planation. It may have been too painful, difficult, or impossible for her to explain. Mary Ellen Manz, her superi-
or in Chillán, had said that Carla was "growing by leaps
and bounds," and Carla's announcement was painful for
her. The suddenness of the decision and Carla's refusal to
discuss it made Mary Ellen wonder if she had failed Carla in some way or whether she should have encouraged earlier discussion with Carla of some discontent. Carla wrote
to Pat, "I haven't been able to open to too many people—in
fact about that decision, NO ONE. But now it's made and I
won't look back. I'm going back to Chillán next week to say
goodbye. Buzeta will be my home from March on."

***

Since 1953 San Juan de Dios parish had served Santiago's población Buzeta, a working class area in a tough

neighborhood near a slaughterhouse and one of the oldest red-light districts. The convent was adjacent to the school; the parish church was blocks away. In addition to the large school, the parish provided a staff of social workers and sponsored neighborhood health clinics, a workers' co-op, youth groups, and a mothers' club. Carla began teaching sixth grade.

A few months after she settled in Buzeta, in the spring of 1972, Carla met David Meissner, a journalist from Milwaukee, an investigative reporter for the *Milwaukee Journal* who was traveling through several Latin American countries with letters of introduction from major businesses and banks in the Milwaukee area. A contact from the U.S. Catholic Conference recommended the Maryknollers as the most knowledgeable people for him to talk to. When Meissner arrived in Santiago only to find all hotel rooms filled and his reservation bumped by a meeting of the UN Committee on Trade and Development, it was quickly arranged that he could stay at the Maryknoll rectory until a hotel room was available.

Over dinner at the rectory he was seated across from Carla and noticed her Midwestern accent. She was thrilled to meet someone from Wisconsin, and they continued their conversations over two or three evenings. He met several notable individuals while touring Latin America that year but later said, "She's the only one who made such an impression on me that I wanted to stay in touch." While in Chile he learned that many people had lost confidence in Allende—inflation was already at fifty percent. Carla told him that it was difficult for the poor to obtain jobs unless they had a membership card in the party and that the sisters had trouble getting food and supplies for the women they served. She was most appreciative when Meissner offered to call her mother upon his return to the United States.[22] Carla wrote to me about meeting Meissner and encouraged me to contact him.

In October 1972 a national truckers' strike, covertly orchestrated by opposition to Allende in order to create chaos and unrest, further disrupted the lives of all Chilean citizens. Frustration grew and the population became even more polarized. On the right, people were convinced Allende must be defeated. On the left, some supported Allende; others, frustrated that change was too slow, began to seize factories and farms. The Popular Unity coalition was no longer unified.

During 1973 Carla worked closely with Skip Flynn, a Maryknoll seminarian who arrived in Chile that January and moved to Buzeta after a brief rural assignment. Carla greeted him saying, "So you're Skip Flynn, the seminarian with the beautiful blue eyes that all the sisters are talking about—you're coming to work with me in Buzeta!" They began team-teaching seventh- and eighth-grade religion classes. He credited her for filling in gaps in his Spanish. He also sympathized with her efforts at "father formation" as long overdue, since some of the clergy were far too removed from the poor—they lived well, ate well, and golfed at the country club when they chose.[23]

In addition to her teaching, Carla worked with a prayer group of Chilean Air Force wives, helping them prepare their children for first communion. She believed it was important to work not only with the poor but also with the well-to-do. Yet she was still restless, drawn to live more closely with the poor. In the spring of 1973 she eagerly accepted an invitation from Connie Pospisil, MM, to move into población La Bandera with Connie and Mary Tracy, MM. For several months she split her time between La Bandera and Buzeta, commuting almost two hours by bus to complete her teaching and her work with the prayer group. By this time her bronchial problems were so much worse that she needed weekly medical treatments. And it did not help that she had resumed smoking.

CHAPTER FOUR

La Bandera

POBLACIÓN LA BANDERA was a settlement of 80,000 inhabitants on the southern outskirts of Santiago. It had been established before 1970, during the administration of President Frei. By the time Carla moved to La Bandera in 1973, Allende's government had developed additional poblaciónes surrounding the city to accommodate Chile's poorest rural peasants. Most of La Bandera's residents had only a grade-school education—or less—and had moved there from the country or smaller towns in hopes of finding work. In 1973 residents faced chronic miseries of hunger and unemployment; many sought refuge in cheap Chilean wine. In spite of their frustrations and anger, the residents often possessed a spirit of solidarity and sharing with one another.

When Carla arrived in La Bandera, she joined Connie and Mary in the small wooden house they had built. It had three tiny bedrooms, a one-room living-dining-kitchen area, a real floor, and the luxury of running water and indoor plumbing.[1] Most población residents got their water from spigots in pipes that ran down the middle of the unpaved roads. Many lived in shacks raised off the ground by cement blocks or wood, and a few shelters sat directly on the ground.

Jessie Poynton, MM, who then lived in another Santiago población, described the area: "There were few trees and in the summer the blazing sun scorched everything and shortened tempers. Then, since its streets were not paved, the earth turned to a fine dust that blew around and grated on

41

everyone's nerves. In winter the streets turned to mud and the people suffered from cold and dampness and hunger."[2]

La Bandera indeed was a tough, grim place, filled with people desperate to survive. Carla instinctively went out to the most destitute—the alcoholics, thieves, hungry children, and lonely elderly. "It was Carla more than anyone else who first became a neighbor to these people who frightened others. Carla made friends with and enjoyed these people—they were the 'poor ole beat-up people' she somehow empathized with," said Connie. Mary remembered Carla as an intense, strong-willed woman who sometimes plowed ahead without thinking and whose intensity could challenge others. In her depressive spells Carla became very quiet, withdrawn inside herself.[3]

By this time Carla radically embraced material poverty for herself and urged it on her fellow missioners. "She always felt we weren't living poor enough," said Connie. Carla "had a very strong call to become poor. She was the only one of our region who didn't have a college degree. She did study in the normal school [to get her teaching license] here in Chile. She felt that the possession of a *cartón* [college degree] would influence her and she would become richer rather than poorer. She always tried to stay away from power, be it money power or 'religious' power. She never liked her physical power. But she did have a very strong moral power for herself and those she met...the morals of Christ from the vision of the poor."

By the summer of 1973 Chile's economy had nearly collapsed, and the already overwhelming suffering of the unemployed and malnourished poor grew even greater. Opposition to Allende now came from all sides. Although he had established many programs to benefit the poor, including housing and health projects, the left was frustrated that reforms were not progressing far enough or quickly enough. The right continued its strong opposition. Positions hardened. A general strike, again orchestrated to foster rebellion and bring down the government, halted the delivery of all consumer goods, including food.

***

In July 1973, in the midst of this political and economic turmoil, Ita Ford, MM, arrived to serve in La Bandera. It was
her first mission assignment, but she had already experienced martial law, curfews, and army tanks in the streets
during her six months at language school in Bolivia.

Carla and Ita became close friends very quickly. Connie
Pospisil described the two women as balancing each other
well: Of different temperaments, they challenged and supported each other, sharing a passion for the poor, a deep
spirituality, and a lively sense of humor.

Psychiatrist Maria Rieckelman, MM, visited Carla and
Ita in La Bandera. She remembered them as bright wom-
en with a whimsical sense of humor who lived their radical
commitment to the poor through their own simple, dedicated lives. Both women, in her view, relied on "deep centers
of solitude" to sustain themselves amid the violence and
horror.[4]

Judy Noone, MM, the author of *The Same Fate as the
Poor*, described them well: "They were opposite and alike.
Carla was outgoing, boisterous, argumentative, large in size
and presence. Ita was retiring, unimposing, listening, petite.
They made an incongruous pair. But what they shared most
deeply was a seriousness about life that touched humor and
felt pain and was impatient with anything less than the truth
or contrary to the kingdom of God. Their love for the people
of La Bandera was something else they shared. Carla's tendency to react impulsively was held in check by Ita's need
to analyze, just as Ita's hesitancy to act until everything was
clear was pushed along by Carla's need to move."[5]

That July, as she witnessed the growing suffering of the
Chilean people, Carol wrote "Lord of the Stone Hearts":

Listen to us now.
We are the dry bones in the desert
who await your command to life.

We are the bent reed and smoldering wick
who await your gentleness.
We are the cautious Zacheus
who get so lost in the limbs
that your call from beneath must be a shout.
You who could roll the rock of death,
roll our rocky hearts.

You who could break Paul's prison bars,
burst our imprisoned hearts.
You who could burn out the fear of the twelve
with fiery tongues,
Brand our callous hide with your spirit.

Cornerstone of creation,
rejected by the builders,
You have become the Keystone of history.
Add us—
to your Divine Skyscraper.

During the summer of 1973 the political and economic situations grew steadily worse. On September 10 Ita's brother, Bill, sent word that their father had died. Ita seriously questioned whether she should visit home or not, especially since she had only begun to settle in her new mission work. Carla strongly urged her to go, telling Ita of her sorrow and distress at not being allowed to attend her own father's funeral.

Ita decided to go and on the morning of September 11, Fr. Tom Maney, MM, and Carla drove into the center of Santiago to purchase Ita's plane ticket. They found the traffic blocked and the streets full of frightened people. When Carla turned on the car radio, they heard President Allende speaking from his office in the Moneda, the presidential palace. He announced that a military uprising had occurred in Valparaiso early that morning and that a coup attempt was in progress. Despite this news, Tom and Carla began walking toward the airline office, which was only a few blocks away. But when they saw tanks in the streets and fighter planes flying low overhead, they turned and ran, dodging and crouching, back to the truck and drove it straight to the Maryknoll sisters' centerhouse.

That morning Hawker Hunter fighter planes made eight bombing runs over the Moneda in twenty minutes, setting the presidential house of government on fire. Planes also bombarded Allende's house, where his wife resided, and destroyed radio stations sympathetic to his government. Tanks and soldiers attacked the Moneda and its central plaza. Speaking on the government radio station before rebels cut it off, Allende vowed to defend his government and not surrender. He encouraged his listeners, saying "I have faith in Chile and its destiny."

But in the swift takeover, Allende died. His surviving ministers were imprisoned. Government radio stations, playing martial music reminiscent of Nazi Germany, announced, "This is the military junta. All must return home." A state of siege was declared and for three days people were not allowed to move outside their homes.

During the first days of the siege, Tom Maney stayed at the sisters' centerhouse. On the fourth day, when travel was again allowed, he drove to La Bandera to bring back Mary Tracy. Together with all the sisters, they held a funeral liturgy for Ita's father. Later, referring to his days at the centerhouse, the priest joked that "they (the sisters) are card sharks...beware!" However, he described his experience with Carla in the first hours of the coup as "most terrifying."

On September 21, when flights were finally allowed, Ita flew home. She arrived in New York deeply shaken by the repression she had just experienced in Chile and distressed and angry that most Americans seemed unaware and unconcerned. She had missed her father's funeral but enjoyed the visit with her mother and family. Mrs. Ford, deeply interested in the mission work of the sisters, corresponded frequently with Ita, routinely sending magazines, art supplies, and books of interest. When Ita left after two weeks, eager to return "home" to Chile, it was with her mother's promise to visit over the Christmas holidays.

Historically, Chileans had taken great pride in their tradition of democracy and the absence of military interference. However, by late summer of 1973 the shortage of basic goods—created by deliberate covert manipulation in order to topple Allende—had increased economic and political tensions to such an extent that many Chileans anticipated civil war. Yet they also expected that order would be quickly restored and that the Christian Democrats, the previous administration, would perhaps return to power.

These expectations were crushed. The military regime of General Augusto Pinochet that came to power as a result of the coup was not short-term; it remained in power until 1990. Nor was it restrained. Curfew rules were brutally enforced—anyone on the streets after curfew could be shot. Each night the sounds of gunfire and machine guns were heard. The regime quickly closed the democratic Congress and banned the Communist and Socialist parties. Soon all political parties were banned. La Bandera and all poblaciónes—which the junta saw as hotbeds of resistance—were raided. Any political activity in them was suspect. People were forbidden to assemble.

In the weeks immediately following the coup, thousands were executed; tens of thousands were detained and tortured. An unknown number "disappeared." By September 22 at least seven thousand prisoners were held in the National Stadium, a huge sports arena.

The most well-known victim of the coup was Victor Jara, the beloved Chilean folk singer and poet who was an active supporter of Allende. He was arrested on the morning of September 12 and detained at Estadio Chile, a smaller sports and performance arena. There he was tortured, beaten, and, on September 15, murdered. During those few days, he led other prisoners in song. And he also began a poem:

How hard it is to sing
when I must sing of horror.
Horror which I am living,
horror which I am dying.
To see myself among so much
and so many moments of infinity
in which silence and screams
are the end of my song.
What I see, I have never seen.
What I have felt and what I feel
will give birth to the moment.

Before Jara had finished writing the poem, his captors came to lead him away to his death. But a friend was able to hide the scrap of paper in his shoe and smuggle it out of the stadium. That unfinished poem, "Estadio Chile," became an international rallying cry.[6]

Pablo Neruda, the noted Chilean poet and Nobel prize-winner, age sixty-nine, was then seriously ill at his ocean home in Isla Negra. News of the coup caused him to fail further. He died on September 23, some say of a broken heart. Thousands turned out for his funeral in Santiago in defiance of Pinochet's orders against assembly. It was the first public protest of the coup.

Arrests soon struck the Maryknoll community. When the coup occurred, many Chileans had immediately burned any books and papers, such as Marxist or socialist writings, which the junta would consider subversive. Possessing them would certainly lead to arrest. Although some Chileans assumed that Americans would be safe from arrest, Skip Flynn, the seminarian and Carla's teaching partner, and Maryknoll Brother Joe Doherty were arrested while retrieving some politically sensitive material and were taken to the National Stadium. Flynn lost fifteen pounds while in detention.[7] With the help of church leaders, the two men were freed after eleven days and immediately flown out of the country.

After Flynn and Doherty were arrested, Carla and Ita went to the stadium every day seeking information about them. With those visits the women began their ministry to the families of the prisoners and the disappeared from La Bandera, a ministry which continued long after the Maryknoll missioners were released.

As Ita's mother had promised, she and Ita's sister, Rene, visited during the Christmas holidays of 1973. Mrs. Ford, who stayed two weeks with the sisters at their house in La Bandera, later told friends that the evenings spent with the sisters were the "most beautiful and peaceful time of my life." She appreciated the simplicity of their way of life, their commitment to the people, and especially the generous hospitality of the poor. On her visit, Mrs. Ford met Carla. They became good friends and lifelong correspondents, sharing an adopted mother-daughter relationship—Carla called her "Grandma Ford."

That Christmas Carla wrote her poem "Dark Earth Still Needs Your Star":

> *Lord of the straw, dumb ox, the rags*
> *forgive our volumes, shows and brags*
> *of knowing who you are.*
> *Draw us to your simplicity*
> *erase our great complicity*
> *dark earth still needs your star.*

Although life in La Bandera had been grim before the coup, it was a terrifying hell afterwards. Deliveries of food, medicine, and services to the población were even more drastically cut. Repression increased everywhere: Curfew violators risked gunshots and machine gun fire. Leaders of the ordinary people—peasants in the rural areas, workers in the cities—were executed, and their bodies were often dumped into rivers, both to dispose of them quickly and to spread terror among the survivors. Families that inquired about a prisoner were often told lies—arrests, executions, and burials were routinely denied.

Many clergy, including foreign missioners, were staunch supporters of human rights, and the junta was especially suspicious of the foreigners, regarding them as outside leftist agitators. Within days of the coup, 150 Catholic priests, nuns, and brothers were forced to leave Chile, and in the following months fifty more were arrested. Altogether, 380 clerics, 314 of them foreign missioners, left in the first two years after the coup.[8]

On September 19, 1974, Fr. Joan Alsina, a Spanish priest who was a chaplain at San Juan de Dios Hospital in Santiago and also active in the workers' movement, was arrested and executed. Two other priests were known to have died of torture that year. Maryknoll priest Dick Sammon, who worked in a rural area, later said, "I thought I was going to die. I experienced a tremendous amount of repression in 1975–76 as a result of trying to organize the campesinos. I was getting shot at and my house was searched." Prisoners taken from the jail were executed at the local bridge, he said, and "people came into the parish crying, 'Padre, the bridge is soaked in blood.' "[9]

In La Bandera, a priest was arrested on a charge of aiding extremists after arms were planted in the tabernacle of his small chapel. Another neighbor of Carla and Ita, a priest who had taught Marxism at the Pontifical Catholic University in Santiago, was expelled.

Residents of poblaciónes were particularly suspect, as if being poor was in itself subversive. Troop battalions with tanks and machine guns repeatedly rolled into La Bandera at dawn to round up men and boys on the football field. Some were taken, tortured, and released; others disappeared. It was commonly believed that the soldiers were given alcohol and drugs before they went on their raids.

Liz Gilmore, SHCJ, who then lived in La Bandera, described a neighbor's horrendous experience during a raid: When the soldiers broke into her house, this simple woman mistakenly asked them for help. "You've got to do something about my husband—he's always drinking too much," she said. They instantly shot him dead.[10]

After the coup, Carla continued her work with mothers in Buzeta to help prepare their children for first communion, even though the husbands of many of the women were career members of the Chilean Air Force. She was convinced not only of the importance of serving people regardless of their politics or social status, but, above all, of the importance of faith and the value of the sacraments as sources of strength and consolation. She sent Maryknoll the story of Nalda, one of the Buzeta mothers, to illustrate the coup's impact on all Chileans. Nalda's husband had suffered a severe nervous breakdown after his superiors ordered him to kill fellow Chileans. Nalda was bitter toward the church, but she nevertheless asked a priest to take communion to her hospitalized husband. At first she refused communion for herself, but after much encouragement she received the sacrament. Carla believed that Nalda was greatly helped by this return to her faith: "Now I would say, in spite of the fact that her husband is in a mental hospital, she isn't alone adding to her bitterness but living with hope and the life of the Word of God."

Miguel Cruz, a resident of La Bandera, worked closely with Carla and Ita. Carla saw his leadership potential and recruited him to help organize the community and, later, to supervise projects, including the building of a chapel. Miguel and his family still reside in their small, well-kept home in La Bandera. He fondly remembered Carla, calling her "The Sergeant," the one in charge with her detailed plans and task assignments. He also recalled the fear and frustration of life under the military regime. On one occasion he watched Carla confront the soldiers who were rounding up men and boys. She insisted that these were innocent men and boys who had done nothing wrong and that they should not be arrested. She was positive that the soldiers would respect her religious status and honor her plea. Thirty years later Miguel sobbed as he described how the armed men pushed Carla away and shoved her to the ground. She would have persisted, Miguel said, had not he and others held her back.[11]

Anyone associated with helping the poor, including church personnel, was suspect. At least once the threats against the nuns were so serious that they split up to stay overnight in different houses. Assemblies were still forbidden. During one evening meeting for young men and boys at the sisters' house, they heard soldiers in the street outside; everyone inside froze in terrified silence. Fortunately, the soldiers moved on.

Raids on the población were always carried out in a deliberately frightening manner in order to intimidate and terrify the victims. Soldiers and police broke through doors, hacked mattresses and other furnishings, and destroyed anything they chose. The sisters were subjected to the same terrorizing tactics as the poor. Their little house was raided at least three times—by army soldiers, by the air force, and finally by the plainclothes secret police of DINA (National Intelligence Directorate). On this last raid, the most frightening and nerve-wracking, six armed men crashed in and ransacked every room. The experience was particularly harrowing for the three women because they were afraid that the intruders would discover university textbooks of a political nature that they had hidden in a suitcase on a high closet shelf. Fortunately, the books were not found.[12]

As the regime continued its campaign of terror, the atmosphere of violence and fear damaged everyone. Carol Marie McDonald, who had arrived in Chile in 1963 and lived in Santiago during the coup, said: "We had no idea of the psychological or spiritual effects of trauma, and each one of us reacted in different ways to danger, to terror. We were not skilled in helping or supporting each other. I think the only 'normal' reaction many times would be rage, flight or depression." Like many others who lived through those traumatic times, she said it was only when she visited home—

and experienced the absence of gunfire, machine guns, and terror—that she finally realized the tension she had been living with.[13]

To convey the experience of terror and the mutual support within the La Bandera community, Ita wrote "Try to Imagine" and sent it to many friends and colleagues. Here are excerpts:

> *Try to imagine* a company of approximately 100 soldiers and about two dozen FBI agents surrounding a working-class neighborhood of 2,000 families at dawn. No one may enter or leave. All men and boys over fourteen years are summoned to a nearby football field, lined up. Any man who has something recorded against him in the last ten years is taken. Also taken are some with names similar to those with records, as well as others for being "suspicious." All fall into a general category of "delinquents."

> *Try to imagine* the wives and mothers milling around the edge of the field from eight in the morning until one in the afternoon...and being told from time to time to return to their homes.

> *Try to imagine* the children frightened by the soldiers with machine guns standing at the corners and accompanying the FBI men to each house. Some begin to cry, "Daddy, don't let the soldiers take you away."

> *Try to imagine* FBI agents entering your home to do a thorough search without any reason given. One has an iron pipe in his hand. They intend to find something they don't like. And of course they do.

> *Try to imagine* each of these things and make it as personal as possible because it is real. It has happened to us. What would you do? How would you react? From whom would you get the strength to face up to this evil, this terror? This is the third time that the soldiers have come.

> Would there be camaraderie among the men in your neighborhood as they walked together to the field,

sharing cigarettes and joking words to keep up each other's spirits?...

Would the women be equally, if not more, solicitous of each other? Would they be so outgoing in their fear as to say, "I'm not worried about my own family, but the neighbor's?" Would they encourage the more nervous to keep busy and distract themselves? Would their faith be the faith of the poor and oppressed who have no "connections," no "pull," but who must rely solely on the mercy and love of God? If you saw your husband taken away, could you say with complete confidence, "I have faith that God will bring him home?" Would your neighbors come to "accompany you" as you waited to learn just what might be the charge against your husband? Would small groups meet a few days later to share how they felt, and then thank God for all those who had returned home and ask for his comfort and support for those still detained and for their families?

We hope so. The only way you and your neighbors could face up to and overcome arbitrary "fishing expeditions" and organized terror is by being very concerned for each other and by having a deep faith not in the judicial process or man's justice, but in a God who cares for His people....We are privileged to have shared this, to know and feel a little of the suffering of the powerless, of those without voice. And we want to share it with you because our neighbors are your neighbors. (Luke 10:29-37)

Carla sent a copy of "Try to Imagine" to Betty and Jack. Life in Bandera, she wrote, is "hard and real according to the World's standards, but the Lord is very generous to us with the peace and joy that the world can't give. I just love working in this direct apostolate. I learn so much from the beautiful poor, simple people with whom I'm privileged to live and work."

***

In January 1974, four months after the coup, the Maryknoll sisters in Chile held a four-day assembly to discern their role within the new political situation. Ita was chosen to make a presentation to the group. In "Thinking About Our Common Call," she noted: "We are a people who not only live in time but in an age of accelerated change...Understanding the true meaning of our call and reading the signs of the times will enable us to adapt to the word of God in a new and changing age, and to do so in peace and in union with each other. Can we say to one another, 'I trust you. I believe in your good intentions. I know the Spirit works in you as he does in me'? Clarifying our common call, then, just might be re-clarifying our own individual faith experience of Christ and our own response to the Spirit's call within us."

The assembly did not produce a unified vision on the role of missioners; rather, it made differences among the participants clear. After the assembly Ita wrote candidly to a friend: "It was very revealing. We could arrive at no common outlook on the events preceding and following September 11. What it showed is how we come to identify with the people with whom we live and work, and since we are in several different situations, we take on the colorings, even without realizing it. Maybe we are not as divided as a group of Chileans might be, but we reflect it to a certain point."[14]

Writing about the conflicts within the religious community that mirrored those among the Chileans themselves, Carla said that she felt bad about "the testimony of disunity and yet the Lord has his reasons. One thing I see is that the people, in all of this, are coming to see that priests and religious are (1) not God, (2) are very human, and (3) are limited and needy just like the rest of the *raza* [all people]. I'm coming to see more and more the crazy fantastic mandates that Jesus left us—so many slogans that we grew up with are so contrary to the Beatitudes."

For many years the leaders of the Catholic Church in

Chile had shown a strong commitment to human rights and especially to the poor. Cardinal Raul Silva had always reached out to the poor and dispossessed. When he was appointed archbishop of Santiago in 1961, he led the way, joined by Bishop Manuel Larrain of Talca, to turn over diocesan lands to landless farm workers—years before the agrarian reform efforts of President Eduardo Frei in 1964–70.

After the coup Cardinal Silva visited the thousands of Allende supporters and activists held prisoner in the stadium. On September 13 he and fellow bishops issued a public statement condemning the bloodshed and reprisals. Silva had been close to the Christian Democrat party, and although he did not support efforts to blend Christianity and Marxism, he had established a somewhat trusting relationship with President Allende.

The Chilean church leadership provided a bulwark of solidarity for the missioners and others concerned for justice. "Chile has a hierarchy that stands up for the little people," Carla wrote to a friend. By early 1974 Silva had established a strong ecumenical Committee for Peace—the Comité. Its large staff of lawyers, social workers, and medical teams documented arrests, disappearances, and torture. Its programs included farm co-ops, health clinics for the poor, and soup kitchens for malnourished children. In April 1974 the bishops issued "Reconciliation in Chile," their first significant criticism of the regime; it called for the re-establishment of constitutional human rights and especially opposed the mistreatment of prisoners and the use of torture.

Even the *comedores*, the dining rooms organized by the Comité that served hundreds of malnourished young children one meal a day, were forbidden by the Pinochet regime as Marxist endeavors. "Anyone who has asked a neighbor to give food for the soup kitchen is marked. Anyone who has helped a priest or taken part in the church programs…is marked. Those who are union activists or members of political parties have long since been eliminated. They were shot, have disappeared, or are rotting in jail. Now the danger lies in being identified with the church or with some project of neighborly solidarity."[15]

Despite the authorities' opposition, comedores sprang up as cooperative projects in the poblaciónes, usually starting in someone's backyard. The mothers of the children organized, prepared, and served the meals themselves. They begged food and donations from more prosperous parishes. In La Bandera the sisters gradually established a partnership with a group of wealthier women, not only to recruit donations but to bring the two groups of women together.

Carla worked hard for the comedores. She wrote me of a wonderful Christmas party that the wealthier women gave at one comedor: They served the mothers of the población so that "these beat-up ladies were queens for a day." The población mothers were asked what coming to the dining room meant to them, and Carla, touched by their replies, wrote: "Their answers were JEWELS!" One woman wrote, "For me the dining room has returned my humanity. Before I felt like an animal just trying to exist—now I've discovered friendship with the other women and I'm able to talk to my husband as a person and not just as a worker who provides for us." Another said, "When I came to the dining room I was afraid I'd feel humiliated, but I risked that for food for my children. However, I discovered what brotherhood really is."

***

All missioners relied on an active faith and prayer life in order to cope with the challenges they faced. Liz Gilmore said that in Chile, with so much misery around you, "If you didn't have a strong life of prayer, it's more than you can take."[16] Many sisters have described Carla as deeply prayerful. She carried on a constant conversation with her Divine Circus Master, digging deep for direction as to how to serve. Ita often joined her in her daily prayers, which included kneeling for hours, sometimes as late as 2 a.m., in the chapel. The chapel was simply a specially designated

area in the middle of their small house and it became un-
comfortably cold in the middle of the night. Both women
relied on a weekly retreat with a spiritual advisor and fasted
regularly on bread, water, and tea.

Carla's spiritual advisor was Padre Pedro Perez, OSB.
She visited him regularly at the Benedictine monastery, carrying her well-worn Bible under her arm, prepared to challenge Scripture interpretations with him. The monastery,
set in the hills overlooking Santiago, was an oasis of natural and man-made beauty. The views were spectacular. Of
the chapel, Carol Marie McDonald noted, "The fascinating
thing was the light. Openings pierced at different angles in
the walls in such a way that there was a constant shifting of
light patterns, according to the position of the sun. The light
was exquisite!"[17] Carla's sessions with Padre Perez provided a respite from the tensions of life in La Bandera. The long
bus ride followed by the walk into the hills also brought its
own peaceful reward.

Ministry meant not simply preparing catechists but also
encouraging everyone to use their talents in service of the
community. In weekly meetings that included prayerful reflections as well as practical efforts to solve the ever-present
problems, the sisters worked to build base Christian communities—small, grassroots groups whose members often shared leadership. Carla and Ita were available day and
night to respond to the urgent needs of the poor, to accompany them as they faced the challenges and nonstop crises of their daily lives: lack of work, hunger, anger, fear, injustice. It was a constant struggle simply to keep everyone
alive. Jessie Poynton, MM, wrote, "Carla and Ita walked the
streets of the capital with the worried expression their people wore, always involved in the same struggle for life, always imploring God's enlightenment and help, always committed to the people living in poverty."[18]

Carla often dragged sisters who worked at the Santiago centerhouse out to the población so they wouldn't forget "the real people." Shirley Duane Alveal, MM, then Regional Superior at the centerhouse, visited Carla and Ita

often and greatly admired the work they were doing. She described them as "ahead of their time...totally committed to the people, radical about the Gospel." In her opinion the two women shared a strong vision of service and "the Gospel came out of them as easy as if they'd been personally walking with the Lord." When Shirley decided to leave Maryknoll and then to marry, she confided first in Ita and Carla. She credited Carla's push—her willingness to confront problems—with nudging her to spend time in prayerful discernment and then to discuss her decision more openly within their community.[19]

The missioners faced constant pressures and challenges in the dangerous political environment. In January 1974 Ita wrote, "The tension between church and state keeps us all honest. You have to make decisions, even though they won't be popular, and can easily be twisted. So we muddle along."[20]

That same year Carla's report to Maryknoll described the poverty and sharing in población La Bandera: "I continue to learn from our gorgeous people. I look at my values of security, cemented in me by years of thrift and hard work and getting ahead, and lay them next to the values I see here—hard work for barely enough for the day, due to the yoke of oppression that lies heavily on the shoulders of the poor. If they lived with our values, they'd soon drown under the tides of despair. It seems to me that the Christian way of sharing can only become a reality with and in the surroundings of the poor. What little bit one family may have obtained today is constantly being used or needed by another who doesn't have today but who shared yesterday—be it a meal or a cup that is one extra for my family but makes up the difference for a family who doesn't have enough."

Carla yearned for more news of her family. Betty kept in touch through brief notes, often accompanied by donations, but she was never one to write lengthy letters. In August 1974 Carla pleaded:

> It's been so long since I've heard from you. I wonder how are you? What has happened this summer?

Mama writes about once a month now with very little in her letters. Gene wrote once but other than that you guys could all be moved, sick, sad, in the poor house or on 5th Avenue for all I know.

I just thought I'd mention that altho I'm far away, I still think about you and remember you to the Lord. It's not much I ask, just a letter to say you really are! Sometimes I feel badly that our family is so dispersed—myself perhaps the most removed—yet here I really know what friendship is, what it means to be close to people even tho far away for long periods of time. Since I have the privilege of seeing this and experiencing it with friends, I say, why can't it be among brothers and sisters who do have a bond in blood and beliefs? Maybe I look for too much from the family that always went its own way. You, Betty, are the only one that I see, visit, and try to keep up some kind of ties. I'm glad—I guess that's why I feel close enough to rant and rave like this. Don't worry about me—I haven't flipped—I just thought I'd express what runs thru my mind and heart once in awhile.

In 1974, struggling with the tension, terror, and dire poverty of life in La Bandera, Carla turned to psychological counseling with Teresa Corquera, a therapist in Santiago, to grapple as well with the problems rooted in her relationship with her family. She wrote to Karen Peterlin, her friend from the noviate, "I'm getting help...towards feeling, knowing, being whole, watered with so many tears. Thanks be to God everyone is very understanding. I need healing and I know Our Father is not absent." She struggled with spells of depression and, as her fellow sisters knew, with the lifelong heartache of feeling unwanted and rejected, as if disowned, by her mother. Her counseling continued for several years and she vowed to some sisters that she would not cut her hair until she was through with it. Her therapist used Carla's poetry and artwork in her university counseling classes.

In addition to her emotional wounds, Carla was coping

physically with worsening bronchial problems. By now Ita
had learned to provide the recommended medical treatments
by pounding on Carla's back. Later, Carla joked that her
"beat-up old ladies" laughed at her celibacy because she was
always cold, saying she needed a husband to keep her warm.
She had burned three heavy woolen habits by standing too
close to the fireplace in her early days in Chile, and she said
she believed that hell would be a place of cold, not fire.

Carla wrote many poems, her own form of journaling,
during her years in Chile. Those written in the months following the coup reflect some of her struggle toward an au-
thentic self:

This Is the End, Heart

This is the end, heart!
From now on, you are alive.
You feel—do you hear me?

You feel as the earth feels the rain,
As the cement feels the hammer,
Just a tiny bit at first...a tiny bit.

That's all I ask you.
That's all I plead.
That's all I cry.

Now I pray, heart,
And you pray, too!
Are we so separate, mind and you?

Go or Stay

What strange and foolish thing we say
mouthing "go" when we mean "stay."
We ask the question "How are you?"

longing to be answered, "Who?"
We seek the ugliest card to deal
to frighten away the hand to heal.
We blow out jokes like curling smoke
then shy away when many choke.

Our mouth is present to a few
the heart, Lord, is still far, it's true.
Will one day the two coincide—
what dollies out, and what's inside?

***

In 1974 Carla wrote to Maryknoll: "So many times it's heard among the people in our occupation—'I want to give, but I've learned so much and received so much.' I say the same phrase, but what is it that I've learned? One of the hardest lessons in life for me has been the commuting of ideas and ideals from the mind into my way of acting and being."

She then told the story of Señora Rosa, who came with her five children to the comedor because her family had no food. Rosa had not registered the children's birth certificates with the proper authorities, which meant they would never be able to attend school. Carla tried many times to encourage Rosa to register them and even offered to go with her, but Rosa did nothing. Finally, Carla issued an ultimatum—register your children or they will lose their places in the dining room.

> That evening other mothers came to my house. They said to me, "You are always saying that the right to eat comes from God. How can you take that right away just because someone doesn't do what you want them to do?"

> That simple statement of a profound truth, spoken in friendship and sincerity, taught me volumes. They were right, very right, and I was very wrong. I

admitted that I was wrong. Sra. Rosa continued to go to the dining room until her husband found a poor job.

I was blind to her own undernourished state, which leaves one more than somewhat apathetic. I could only see the need for the children, which perhaps was more my own need to have her comply with regulations. This simple incident taught me a lot about how I say I respect the needs of the people but I'm only one person who has a lot of blind spots and I need the whole church to help me.

It's humbling and joyful to know that evangelization is going on within the Church. I have come to see that of the poor I have come to share life with, I am perhaps one of the poorest. Of the oppressed to whom I have been sent to teach liberation, perhaps I am the most oppressed. And learning this, I'd say I've learned a lot, wouldn't you?

Carla's spirits dimmed as she witnessed the unrelenting suffering around her. Hunger, joblessness, and disease were exacerbated by helplessness, hopelessness, and the bleak fear induced by the terrorizing regime. Yet she and Ita worked tirelessly to support the people and face challenges together with them.

Confronted by crises, Carla could be a focused realist. When Ceci Vandal, MM, was visiting the población, the people found their electricity suddenly cut off. Ceci was amazed to see Carla go right to work to gather the people. "No time for tears now," Carla said. "We'll cry later—now we have to strategize." Ceci viewed Carla as "living fully what she believed," with complete honesty and a drive to achieve total poverty for herself. "She had a phobia," said Ceci—she feared that she could never be poor enough. In Ceci's opinion, Carla's talk of a heart of stone was her way of being hard on herself, of always trying to be more loving, more giving, and never feeling that she succeeded enough.[21]

On January 4, 1975, the *Appleton Post Crescent* featured a story and picture on Carla's work with the head-line, "Appleton Nun Finds Beauty among Poor in Chile." The story was based mainly on letters Carla had sent to her mother in which she spoke strongly of the generosity of the poor in the face of their great adversity: "Whenever they have more than they need, they share it with their neighbors who may not have enough that day. They enjoy their children and watch them play. Celebrations are important. A good time helps them forget their pain." Carla's letters home emphasized the natural beauty of Chile, springtime flowers, children enjoying the wind and flying their handmade kites. In one she added a special postscript to her mother (not included in the newspaper article): "I do thank the Lord for life, for you, for my being here and all He's given me."

Since the Chilean government censored mail, Carla's letters did not describe the complete scope and danger of the regime. However, a flyer sent out of Chile with the mother of a sister there made clear the political situation and the newspaper story also quoted from that: "About 100 soldiers surrounded the working class neighborhood. No one could enter or leave. All men and boys were summoned to a field nearby, lined up according to alphabetical order in order to determine whether they might have any type of police re-cord...anything from traffic accidents to serious crimes."

What kept Carla—and Ita—going in the midst of this at-mosphere of crisis and despair? First, their genuine love and compassion for the "poor beat-up ol' people" in such des-perate need. Then, their reliance on deeply prayerful con-versations with, in Carla's words, the Divine Circus Mas-ter. And, not least, the support and strength they drew from their friendship. As the terror and violence of the regime continued, Carla's reaction was to pray more. She began to visit Padre Pedro Perez, her Benedictine advisor in the hills, more frequently.

At an Easter Sunday celebration at the Maryknoll sis-ters' centerhouse, Carla and Ita met Sheila Cassidy, a Brit-ish physician who had arrived in Chile in 1971. (Sheila's journey on a cargo boat had differed considerably from

Carla's earlier voyage. Sheila brought with her many of her treasured belongings, including thirty-three pieces of hand luggage—with more stored in the hold—and Winston, her pet chow.) Troubled and frightened for the safety of a friend who had been arrested by DINA, Sheila went to the Benedictine monastery that was Carla's favorite oasis for Easter Sunday Mass. There she met Becky Quinn, who invited her to join the Maryknoll sisters at their Easter celebration.

The Maryknoll women totally punctured Sheila's preconceived notions of nuns. These women dressed in slacks, not religious habits, and were a jolly, joking group. They were strong, independent, faith-filled, and exuberant. Sheila was especially drawn to Carla and Ita, with whom she shared an interest in art and literature, and to the work that they were doing in La Bandera.

Sheila later credited the Maryknoll sisters with leading her to a rebirth of faith. Her experience was similar to that of the distinguished journalist Penny Lernoux, who wrote, "I owe a special debt to Maryknoll because it was through your missioners in Chile that I regained my Catholic faith. [They] showed me a different church—the church of the poor. The experience changed my life, giving me new faith and a commitment to tell the truth of the poor to the best of my ability. There is a saying in this church of the poor: 'You make your path by walking it.' But I walked a path that your people had already made."[22]

Sheila, Carla, and Ita quickly became good friends. They began visiting each other weekly—sharing prayers, liturgies, meals, and socializing—either in La Bandera or at Sheila's home. Sheila remembered Ita and Carla as "special firebrands—they were enormously strong."[23]

Sheila was deeply impressed by Carla and Ita's dedicated work in La Bandera and by their living with and as the poor. On her first visit to their población, she noted the huge difference between the sisters' way of life and her own:

> Their house was in the middle of a row in the center of the población and was only a little better finished than those which surrounded it. The plank walls

inside were unpapered and unpainted, though gaily decorated with folk art and sketches done by Anna. [Since the regime was still in power when she wrote, Cassidy gave pseudonyms to the sisters who were still there: Anna was Carla, Frances was Ita.] They had just what they needed for their life and work in this particular place and no more....The most important part of their work, however, was the simple fact of their presence in the población. Of their own volition three American women were sharing the day-to-day living conditions of poor Chileans. These were not pious foreign missionaries coming in to preach a message of brotherly love and then returning to their comfortable American-style house, but educated young women who lived in a little wooden house like they did, who traveled on foot and by bus as they did and who shared their bread and their friendship and their talents with those who asked. This indeed was a mystery and it spoke more powerfully of the love of God than a thousand sermons.[24]

The Maryknoll sisters introduced Sheila to the large community of priests and nuns working in Santiago—more than forty North American religious women missioners lived in the Santiago area. Sheila appreciated finding English-speaking friendship with the Columban Fathers, who happened to be her close neighbors on the next street. Soon she was pitching in to provide medical treatment for various missioners, often for hepatitis or typhoid. In June 1975 she was asked to work in a new clinic, one of several established by the Comité for Peace, in población El Salto. There she struggled to meet the crushing needs of the starving and unemployed, many of them fearful for family members who had been arrested or disappeared.

While working in Santiago hospitals, Sheila had seen that gunshot victims were presumed to be rebels and were executed on the spot or disappeared. So when a Chilean priest called in October 1975 to ask if she would treat a man with bullet wounds, she agreed, presuming that the worst that could happen to her would be deportation. The victim in hiding was a key member of the MIR (Revolutionary Left Movement), a political party which had mobilized armed resistance against the Pinochet regime. She visited the man twice before he was given asylum at the Vatican Embassy. The regime's search for him became major news.

Two weeks later, the DINA raided the house where Sheila was visiting an ill religious sister. They killed the maid who answered the door and arrested Sheila at gunpoint. She was blindfolded and driven to Villa Grimaldi, DINA's most important detention and torture center.

The Villa, situated on beautiful grounds on the edge of Santiago, had for decades been a gathering spot for artists, intellectuals, and activists—a center of Chile's intellectual life—before it was taken over by the regime and turned into a place of terror and death.[25]

Sheila was kept in solitary confinement and tortured until she broke down while being interrogated about the identity and location of those who harbored or arranged asylum for the MIR members. Eventually she was transferred to Tres Alamos, another detention facility, where she was allowed visitors, including the British consul working for her release.

On her first visiting day Sheila was thrilled to see Carla and Ita arrive. They visited regularly thereafter. Any gifts they carried—fruit, chocolate, sweaters, personal supplies, sewing materials, colored pencils, books of poetry, a prayer book—were first inspected by guards. Priests were forbidden to bring the Eucharist, so on every visit the nuns smuggled in the host, carefully concealed (once in Carla's bra). The women sat on the lawn to talk and share their unconventional liturgies, watched by the guards.

Carla's humor erupted even in this stark setting. Sheila had talked in their earlier prayer gatherings of how hard it would be for her to live simply. She had prayed not to be so attached to her creature comforts—her house, her dogs, her books. Remembering this, the women laughed together when Carla said, "Well, He took you at your word, didn't He?" The women prisoners worked on sewing or art projects to make gifts for their families. Sheila toiled for many hours to painstakingly carve five crosses from soup bones and she gave two of them to Ita and Carla.

Once British officials were allowed to see Sheila, they worked quickly to arrange her release and safe exit from the country. On December 29, 1975, she flew to England. For brief moments as she approached the plane, she waved madly to her friends on the airport observation roof—Carla, Ita, Jane Kenrick, RSM, and many others who had gathered to see her departure. Once Sheila was safely on British soil, the British government strongly denounced the government of Chile for their "brutal, uncivilized treatment of a British subject." Chile denied the charges. Consequently, on January 12, 1976, Britain withdrew its ambassador from Chile.

Sheila Cassidy's ordeal received international media attention that exposed the tragic situation in Chile to the entire world. *Newsweek, Time,* and the *New York Times* gave the story prominent coverage.

Sheila's story revealed the tense face-off between church and state regarding human rights and torture, and the protection of the MIR leaders precipitated a confrontation between the regime and the religious community. Several of those who helped the MIR leaders were priests and nuns, members of the ecumenical Comité. Pinochet alleged that those on the committee were Marxists who endangered the country and he demanded that Cardinal Silva close it down. Silva dissolved it on December 31, 1975, and the next day established a replacement, the Vicariate of Solidarity, under the direct auspices of the Santiago Archdiocese. The Vicariate's mission was the same as the Comité's—to defend human rights, document and protest violations, and provide services for the poor.

Sheila's arrest and interrogation also had serious consequences for the Maryknoll sisters and others in Santiago who had helped the rebels. Three nuns sought by the secret police for their possible involvement in, or knowledge of, the asylum given to the two MIR leaders spent several fear-filled days in hiding before finding safe haven in embassies. The search for political asylum was complicated because it was extremely difficult to ascertain who—in any position, even on the staff of a sympathetic embassy—could be trusted.

When police came to search the Maryknoll centerhouse, Ceci Vandal had the presence of mind to ask them to wait until her group finished their liturgy. During the Kiss of Peace, as the waiting police looked on, the sisters passed each other the message, "Beware, the phones are now tapped."[26]

In addition, because of the large number of missioners in Chile and the similarity of many of their names (e.g., Jean, Joan, Jane, Janet, Jo), the DINA was confused at times about whom to arrest. According to Jane Kenrick, "Even if they had all spoken the truth it would have been difficult to unravel the tale and explain why one nun who was a Sr. of the Holy Child had been spending a week with some friends of the Notre Dame community but was no longer in the same house because she had gone to spend the night with a friend who was a Sr. of Mercy in the house of a Maryknoll sister because the Maryknollers were out of Santiago for the weekend at a conference being held in a retreat house run by the Society of the Sacred Heart! It is small wonder that one officer cried out in disgust, 'Nuns, priests, bishops, it's all too much!' "[27]

***

On November 8, 1975, just a week after Sheila's arrest, the headline of a small story in the *Milwaukee Sentinel* captured my attention: "Chile Expels 3 Nuns." The report stated that three nuns from the United States who "allegedly conspired to hide some of Chile's most wanted left-wing guerrillas have flown home after being expelled by the military government. The nuns, Margaret Lipsio of the Maryknoll congregation and Notre Dame members Barbara Nelson and Paula Armstrong, left Pudahuel Airport Friday night bound for Miami, Fla. A crowd of about 200 hostile Chileans shouted at them as they boarded a Braniff International jetliner and tossed small coins as a gesture of insult."

I became deeply frightened for Carla and wrote immediately to Maryknoll to express my concern. In her reply, a representative of Maryknoll said that the Maryknoll sister sought by DINA had been given asylum by the U.S. Embassy in Chile, that the Maryknoll sisters in Chile were as "safe" as possible given the political situation, and that their status as American citizens carried some protection. The letter continued, "It is the people themselves who are the victims of injustice. I am sure Carol would not want anyone worrying about her. She is working and living among people she loves, and she wants to be with them during this time of suffering the Chileans are undergoing at present. Her very presence among them now tells them of her own concern and the concern of the Church for them." All this was true, of course, but I was still worried and I wrote to Carla.

"What a jolly surprise to receive your letter! It made me feel so good when you said you were concerned," Carla replied. "It's kind of warming to know that someone is aware of what's going on. It makes a difference to know that someone might worry." She wrote that she planned to visit the states on furlough in 1976 and hoped that we could get together. She did not expect to arrive in Wisconsin until August. She recommended that I read *The Desert Is Fertile* by Dom Helder Camara and I promptly ordered two copies—for her and for myself. For Carla, and for many, Brazilian bishop Dom Helder's commitment to nonviolence and justice for the poor was a profound inspiration.

Carla had last been home in 1969 and I knew from her letter how much she looked forward to this visit: She had great hopes for reconciliation with her mother. I did not know that she was already feeling worn out and spent, her nerves shattered. Because of the Chilean government's censorship of mail, she said nothing about the terrors of the regime in Chile or of her friendship with Sheila Cassidy, whose story by now had been headlined in major newspapers and the major U.S. news magazines.

Carla's note ended with mention again of David Meissner, the Milwaukee reporter she first met in Chile in 1972. When he traveled to Chile in mid-October 1975 (prior to

Sheila Cassidy's arrest), touring on behalf of the Inter-American Press Association, he had written Carla in advance, to be sure of seeing her again.

This time he had his own hotel room. Carla left a note for him at the hotel, inviting him to visit the sisters' home and giving directions. He took a taxi—with a driver who was nervous about taking him there—to población La Bandera. As he walked around the dirty, dusty neighborhood with Carla and Ita, it was clear to him that the people had great respect and love for these women. It was a tough area, inhabited by some tough-looking individuals, but Meissner was certain that if anyone tried to harm one of the sisters, "there'd be hell to pay from these folks."

He said that at this time the main work of the sisters was the comedores, the soup kitchens that provided one daily meal for malnourished young children and nutrition for pregnant moms. Ita and Carla also spoke of working informally with women through Pro Familia: "We're not telling women not to have children, but to think about when to have children,...because we see so much poverty and suffering, malnutrition and illness...that children cannot reach their potential." Carla was horrified by the large number of babies and young children who died from malnutrition. The sisters served Meissner a meat lunch, which he knew to be a rare treat. He left a donation to support their soup kitchens.

Meissner admired Ita and Carla; he saw that they were both courageous and effective. He recalled Carla as a woman of strength, a leader. When he was leaving, she walked him to a bus stop with strict instructions on which bus to take. He remembered being nervous as he waited for the bus, conspicuously American in his suit and tie.

He and Carla hoped to see each other when she visited Wisconsin in 1976. Upon his return to the States, he fulfilled his promise and called their mothers.[28]

CHAPTER FIVE

The States

CARLA LEFT CHILE ON APRIL 1, 1976; in a letter to me, she joked that April Fool's Day was a good day to start a pilgrimage. Her furlough, two years overdue, was to include a medical checkup, psychiatric counseling, study (for her, a retreat), and a visit home. Her original plans were to be at Maryknoll by early May, spend two weeks with her family in Appleton, attend a Mission Institute in June, make a thirty-day retreat in July, and return to Chile in September. In her report to Maryknoll she said that she would not give any media interviews, as was customary, during her visit "because of our situation in Chile" and described her life in the "very poor marginated población outside of Santiago. My work consists in preaching the Gospel to groups of couples who—for the majority—have never heard it. Also I help coordinate five dining rooms where 400 under-nourished children of the unemployed eat dinner every day."

After years of being in therapy, Carla had gained new empathy for her mother, a woman who not only had a child unexpectedly late in life but, not many years later, suddenly found herself a widow. Carla carried great hopes for their reconciliation. Although over the years Mrs. Piette had apparently at times spoken proudly to others of Carla's religious vocation and mission work, it seems that Carla did not hear of her mother's support.

In her usual style, Carla went home without informing anyone, even her mother, of her exact plans. Had she done so, relatives might have better prepared her. As it was, she arrived unaware that her mother was suffering with serious dementia. Mrs. Piette did not recognize Carla and was unnerved by her presence. In the middle of her first night home, Carla awoke to find a flashlight shining in her face and her mother shouting, "Who are you? What are you doing here? Get out of my house!" Carla, so recently terrified by military raids at gunpoint, was equally traumatized. She fled her mother's house in the dark and walked many blocks to the convent of our old parish, St. Mary's, where she stayed for the remainder of her time in Appleton.[1]

Carla later wrote to Connie Pospisil: "Home was very hard. Mom didn't go to a home but I believe she'll soon have to either go or be taken. I returned a little less than a basket case and have been 'recovering' slowly. As my aunt told me when I was home, I don't know how to work or relate with mentally ill people and I took every nasty thing my mother said personally. So...I'm getting help again and learning once again what it means to be poor and dependent."

It was so difficult to communicate with her mother that Carla cut her visit short. She returned to Maryknoll in New York in time to attend the May 22 ordination of Skip Flynn, her teaching friend from Buzeta. He recalled Carla as "truly broken in spirit" after her visit home. He introduced her to a newly widowed parishioner he was counseling and was moved to see the "two broken and torn women minister to each other."[2]

Carla had written me not to expect her before August, but I was thinking of her often, especially after the news of Sheila Cassidy's ordeal and the expulsion of the three nuns. In late June I dreamed she was at my door. The next day, a Sunday, the phone rang at 5 p.m. "Hi, I'm at the bus depot here—you know, here in Milwaukee—can you pick me up?" I was thrilled to see her.

During her visit, my husband and I learned more about Carla's life in Chile—the atrocities she had witnessed, the daily struggles of the poor and their generosity with each other. She was candid about her own fragile mental health and shattered nerves. She said that there was talk of

Maryknoll opening a new mission in Caracas, Venezuela, and that she was determined to look into the possibility of an assignment there. She spoke of her close friendship with Sheila Cassidy, the details of Sheila's imprisonment and release, and the raids at gunpoint on the sisters' home. Carla was eager to know more about our lives as well, especially since we were both social workers and my husband, Tony, worked with anti-poverty programs in Milwaukee's inner city neighborhoods. She was pleased to know that there were groups in this country, such as the Justice and Peace Center where I volunteered, that were concerned about international human rights and the poor in other parts of the world.

***

Since our freshman year at Marquette, Carla had been especially drawn to Ignatian spirituality. Even while in Chile she continued a subscription to Jesuit Studies and discussed its articles in correspondence with Fr. Ganss. She was thrilled that she would make a thirty-day Ignatian retreat at the Jesuit Retreat House in Oshkosh, Wisconsin. She intended to use the discernment process to decide whether to stay in Chile or to move on, as she hoped to do, to a new mission in Venezuela.

The Oshkosh retreat house lies in peaceful, wooded country on the shores of Lake Winnebago. In July I drove Carla there, knowing that I would see her again after the retreat and her final visit to Appleton.

Beyond the retreat's spiritual benefits of reflection and renewal, Carla found other blessings during those thirty days. One blessing was friendship with another retreatant, Sr. Bernice Fenske, a Holy Spirit Missionary Sister. Bernice wrote of Carla:

> The retreat was a severe strain for her, but the Director [Benno Kornely, SJ] made her several allowances. For example, she was talking Spanish with a Latin American family down the road to help them in their adjustment. I also remember once she "broke down" at

a liturgy. But always she went on. She shared with me her breakdowns in Chile, her rebirths, too. Her concern for the "beat-up ole ladies" was a regular theme in the many times she wrote me. One could tell how she gave of herself so utterly and completely until she was so down that there was nothing left to give. She had a very sensitive soul, a very artistic spirit, and a jolly (she used that word so often) quality that sparkled in her eyes. She talked frequently about poverty and she lived it. She made us aware of the poor and their oppression. But the greatest of all was when she prayed for the oppressors as being the ones most in need, as being really poor.

During the retreat, Carla created a cross-stitched banner with personalized symbols for each retreatant and shared it with the group. At the end of the retreat, a butterfly, a symbol of resurrection, was still incomplete. Bernice said, "Somehow its unfinishedness speaks to me about Carla in a very special way. She never seemed to be finished with anything. In her vision she saw so many areas of need and wanted to be in all of them at once."

The Spanish-speaking family that Carla visited was from El Salvador, and they were delighted to converse with someone in their own language. Four years later the mother went to Benno Kornely for consolation: She was devastated to learn of Carla's death in El Salvador and worried that she might have influenced her to go there.[3]

Another blessing of that time was an unexpected visit with Fr. Ganss. While driving from Winnipeg to St. Louis, he had made a last minute decision to stop at the retreat center. On arrival he was told that one retreatant was a Maryknoll sister who had studied at Marquette—perhaps he knew her? He and Carla corresponded from time to time, but they had not seen each other since 1958 and he had no idea that she was in the country. After Carla's death Fr. Ganss wrote to Maryknoll, "I marveled at the depth, breadth and solidity of her spiritual outlook and how nicely, too, it blended with

her spontaneously cheerful disposition. Her now matured
and experienced spiritual vision was so manifestly the driving force in her life."

At the end of July Carla wrote to Fr. Ganss of her happiness at their accidental meeting and how her time at the retreat house had fulfilled her greatest hopes:

> When I planned my trip home from Chile I could only
> make skeletal plans and then kind of trust in the Lord
> that dreams and desire might fall into these plans. I
> know that sometimes our dreams are kind of simple
> but nonetheless, the Father sees that they are fulfilled.
> I dreamed of seeing you and visiting. I dreamed of
> enjoying a Wisconsin lake and all that Wisconsin of-
> fers—scenery, climate, food and people. I dreamed of
> being filled with beautiful liturgies since so seldom
> we enjoy that in Chile, and I dreamed of getting to
> know some American sisters and hear and learn of
> what they are doing. All these came true by choosing
> 30 days with the Lord.

> Besides all these side gifts this retreat has been a gift
> which I know will continue to give for the rest of my
> life. To come to know Jesus a little bit better each day
> and realize His love for me and what His life means in
> my own life—these mysteries and graces will come
> to nourish me, I'm sure, as I head back to Chile. That
> decision of deciding between Chile and Venezuela
> was hard and yet I'm glad I was here to make it with
> help of a directress and time to discern.

> So once again I say thank you, Fr. Ganss, for let-
> ting the Spirit direct you to Oshkosh and for our jolly
> meeting. I return home now for 10 days to spend with
> my mother and then back to Chile. I feel I can more
> trustfully leave her in the Father's hands after these
> 30 days. Know that I will certainly remember you in
> my prayers, and I ask your blessing on myself as I
> continue this pilgrimage. May we meet again on our
> paths toward the Lord. Peace and joy in the Lord.

The retreat directress, Nancy Vollman, OSU, remembered Carla as a "woman of strength and dedication...willing to sacrifice all for what she thought right. Although she described herself as nerves shattered, at the end of retreat she was joy filled, at peace with her decisions and ready to move on filled with conviction and God's grace. She was a woman of deep prayer and Spirit filled. It was a privilege to know her."[4]

In her discernment process Carla was clearly torn by conflicting desires: to stay in Chile or to leave. She longed for a new beginning but in the end acknowledged her own emotional need for stability and decided to stay. Yet, contradictorily, in her discernment process she included "a chance to die to Chile, friends, work" as a positive reason to leave. Perhaps this ambivalence reflected her fear of becoming too attached.

"In the end I had to say no [to moving] because I'm too weak, needy and I guess you'd say problematic inside to get out of myself," Carla wrote to Connie Pospisil. She listed in detail her insights from the discernment process (which she called her "blood, sweat, and tears"): the pros and cons of going to Venezuela, the pros and cons of not going. She starred the major points where the directress helped her make her discernment more personal and real: "I need community at this time. I'm psychically drained and need a known work and recuperation. I feel a responsibility to community and work in Chile. I'm not the Mother foundress type and can't take a lot of tension."

Connie was then in the States, considering her own decision of whether to return to Chile or take another assignment. Carla seemed hopeful of her return. "Once again I say I support whatever decision you make. Know you are wanted and needed. I'm no prize to live with, yet I believe I can give something to community. The Father is great in His mercy and I believe I'm growing, too."

On July 26 Carla wrote me about the benefits of her retreat and urged me strongly to make a women's retreat in

Oshkosh—"even married women are here, Hansen!" I had asked if she would speak to a group of concerned advocates at the Justice and Peace Center in Milwaukee upon her return, but she declined:

> Well, I'm ending 30 days in the desert with the Lord. A real blessing and kind of hard at times—I guess I'll always be a retard in many ways. That's why He chose me, I say, as Jesus said, "I come not to call the just, but sinners, not the well, but the sick." Anyway, I'd say every nite I went to bed feeling I knew Jesus just a tiny bit more—so for that alone this has been a valuable experience. And of course, to give me the courage to go home once more, to believe in my right to a life different from the traditional Piette life and accept Mama as she is. I believe all that will come.

> I say in all sincerity, my nerves are *shot* after being with my mother and since they aren't too grand to begin with, I just might not be able to do it. Having gone thru military coups, dealing with starving children, and getting psychiatric treatment does take its toll and I accept my poorness in this area. I love talking with you and visiting your mom and dad—I don't think on this trip I can take on groups. By the way (you'll like this) I haven't smoked for over a month. It's warming to me to know there's someone I can talk with here who I feel might feel a bit the same as I do and is doing something about brotherhood in this poor ole beat up world.

Following the retreat Carla again visited her mother and family in Appleton. She attended the fiftieth wedding anniversary of her mother's sister Katherine and her husband, Arnold Laudert. By then Carla urgently wanted to return to Chile. Just as she felt that her family did not understand her mission work, perhaps Carla could not understand or accept their lives. She found it impossible to relate to anyone in her family other than Betty. She told the family that she never wanted to visit the States again—she could not tolerate the consumerism and waste.

In addition to seeing her relatives in Wisconsin, Carla visited Betty and Jack in Michigan and her brother Jim in Georgia. Jim later told Mary Ellen Manz that he and his family found it difficult to relate to Carla when she appeared unannounced on their doorstep, looking like a bag lady. She stayed only briefly and declined their offer of a ride.

While in the States, Carla also visited her old friend Pat Cobb McKenny, who had married a widower with children and now lived in a middle-class area on Long Island. Correspondence between these two close friends had dwindled after Pat left Maryknoll in 1972. Pat recalled that Carla deplored Pat's surroundings as sumptuous excess. Pat said, "She gave me the impression that only the poor were worthy of attaining the kingdom of heaven." The meeting—and their relationship—ended on a strained note. Years later Pat acknowledged that she, too, when she returned home from the extreme poverty of mission life, might have seen the neighborhood she lived in as excessively affluent. Nonetheless, the ending of their long friendship was painful to her.[5]

Carla's radical stance on behalf of the poor might have led her to the conclusion that only by being poor can one gain salvation, or at least that salvation is much more difficult for the rich to attain. Every missioner when visiting the United States after living among the poor experienced culture shock, and Carla's beliefs and attitude may have been more extreme than most.

Sheila Cassidy was at Maryknoll that July, just six months after her Chilean imprisonment, to make a presentation on justice and international human rights. She would have liked to visit with Carla while in the States but realized that Carla needed to stay focused in her retreat.[6] Instead, Carla sent Sheila a Chilean handkerchief, hand-painted with a *copihue*, the Chilean national flower, along with her meditation on Psalm 23:

Waters of Mountains—Waters of God
cleanse us, renew us so shabbily shod.
Rios de Chile, streams of burnt snow
melt us, tow us beyond friend or foe.
Currents so fast, pools deep and clear
tune us, quiet our hearts still to hear.
Lord of the river, God of the stream
teach us your song, our dryness redeem.[7]

When Sheila learned that Carla had died in a river, she immediately recalled this meditation. She treasured a line in a letter that Carla wrote her from the retreat, one that captured Carla's commitment and unique style: "It's a marvelous thing to be on a journey, not knowing where you are going, especially if you trust the cabbie!"

During her last days in Appleton Carla enjoyed dinner with my mom and dad. She found them easy to talk with and had always enjoyed their company, sharing perhaps a cigarette, probably a cocktail, and always good-natured joking. Mom drove Carla halfway to Milwaukee; I met them and took her the rest of the way to the Milwaukee airport.

I remember that Carla carried only one small bag. I remember that, despite my protestations, she insisted on giving me a gift that someone had just given her. I knew she was returning to Chile, but I also knew she was interested in eventually moving on. Nicaragua and El Salvador were definitely mentioned. At the airport we were surrounded—confronted, really—by a group of assertive young people—perhaps Hare Krishna—begging for money. Carla donated with a friendly smile. Then she threw her arms around me in the large Chilean *abrazo*, reminding me that she had learned from Chileans how to be openly affectionate. And off she went, happily toting her one small bag.

Carol on first birthday, one of many photos with her father that day. *Photo courtesy of the Betty Piette Frazier family.*

Carol, age 10, with author, on our way to swim lessons.. *Photo courtesy of the author.*

Piette Family – mother Rose with Carol, brothers Jim and Eugene, sister Betty, and father Jim. *Photo courtesy of the Betty Piette Frazier family.*

Sr. Rose Carol at
Maryknoll, New York,
September 1961.
Photo courtesy of the author.

Sr. Rose Carol
with Chile mission
assignment, Maryknoll
departure ceremony,
August 1964.
*Photo courtesy of
Karen Peterlin.*

With her mother on
home visit before leaving
for Chile, August 1964.
*Photo courtesy of the
Betty Piette Frazier family.*

With her second-grade schoolboys of San Vicente, Chillan, 1966.
Photo courtesy of the Betty Piette Frazier family.

Carla enjoying the countryside of Chile, 1968. *Photo courtesy of the Betty Piette Frazier family.*

Carla and Ita Ford, MM, with residents of *población* La Bandera, 1974. *Photo courtesy of the Maryknoll Mission Archives.*

Carla with mothers and children at a *comedor* soup kitchen, La Bandera, 1976.
Photo courtesy of the Maryknoll Mission Archives.

Carla in joyful reunion with sister Betty on her visit to Chile, November 1978. *Photo courtesy of the Betty Piette Frazier family.*

Carla greeting Ita at Coelemu train station upon Ita's delayed return to Chile, November 1979. *Photo courtesy of the Maryknoll Mission Archives.*

Woman placing floral cross in the river where Carla drowned near San Antonio Los Ranchos, Chalatenango, for annual memorial to Carla, August 23, 2008. *Photo courtesy of the Maryknoll Sisters, El Salvador.*

Villagers of San Antonio Los Ranchos gather at the river for annual memorial to Carla, August 23, 2008. *Photo courtesy of the Maryknoll Sisters, El Salvador.*

Local women view new monument of *Hermana Karla* in community park where Archbishop Romero and Farabundo Martí are honored, San Antonio Los Ranchos, Chalatenango, 2009. *Photo courtesy of Tiempos Nuevos Teatro, El Salvador.*

Gravesite of Sister Carla Piette, MM, in the colorful cemetery of Chalatenango, El Salvador, December 2005. *Photo courtesy of the author.*

CHAPTER SIX

Return to La Bandera

SOON AFTER SHE RETURNED to Chile in September 1976, Carla resumed therapy with Teresa Corquera. She was troubled and torn; the disappointing visit with her mother was a fresh source of pain in their difficult relationship.

She had missed an assembly of sisters while in the States and after her return sent a message to Maryknoll's Regional Governing Board (RGB) to thank them for the many times they had given her personal support, counsel; or a push—whether welcome or not:

> Dear Sisters,
>
> Since I wasn't present at the July assembly, I feel a little "disenfranchised" (more than I usually am, that is). However, since I returned I've been reading the different visions of what the RGB should be and I would like to share mine.
>
> In reflecting on this I think back on my twelve bumpy years in Chile. I say bumpy because I recognize myself as far from the well-rounded, mature religious I'd have a "vision" of being. In my first year I received from the RGB orientation, direction and caring, which I sometimes accepted and also which I rebelled against.
>
> In my years in Chillán the RGB helped me become aware of the whole Church in Chile, my own need for education, and also entered into a few problems which

neither myself nor the local community could solve alone. The members of the Board spent time and energy with us and helped us all to grow up a little bit.

When I went to Santiago, again I received orientation and caring from the RGB. Because of my personal problems they helped me see a bit my own weaknesses and suggested I get professional help, and encouraged me when I didn't always see the best results. They set up meetings along with committees to help my vision grow and be more aware of what's going on in Chile, in the Church and in myself.

Since I've been in Bandera, the RGB has been a big help when there were situations with which I could not cope or didn't know how to confront alone. I've seen them help others who I was not able to help, and they've given me support when I felt pretty beaten-up.

Why do I say all this? Maybe just to say that my vision of the RGB is one of a weaker member of the region who needs someone to help them along the camino. I see them as ordinary beat-up MK Sisters whose call from Community, their talents and the Lord is of service to the Sisters, as I feel called to service of the people in their pilgrimage towards real maturity. Yet I feel that I owe to them what I expect from the people I serve once in awhile—recognition and support.

By 1976 the missioners and anyone affiliated with the Catholic Church faced increased hostility, opposition, and persecution from the Pinochet regime. Ita and Carla developed a "Statement of a Common Vision" to share with fellow missioners:

We are a community of women religious, called to continue the prophetic mission of Jesus, that is: to save, to heal, to bring men to the Father by proclaiming and sharing the 'Good News' of hope and reconciliation to the abandoned by the world and to those who have not had Christ's message proclaimed to them.

As religious in Chile we are challenged to be creative in incarnating the gospel values at this historical moment. As missioners our special charism is to be open to search for new frontiers, collaborating with the local Church's task of liberating evangelization of the entire person.

Carla's Christmas letter in 1976 gave a glimpse of the painful realities of the situation in Chile: "It was so jolly to spend time with you during my time on the 'Northern Continent'...When I returned I found Chile much the same. The release of political prisoners...attributed to Carter... was a jolly sign. However, there are still 383 persons 'disappeared,' and many are from where I work and live. Today is a day of prayer and penance for a solution—at least a definite answer to the families. It took me awhile to get over the trauma of home and mama. However, with help and understanding I feel I'm beginning to be my old self again."

***

Ita and Carla's relationship was strong, so strong that they were able to challenge, as well as to support, one another. Marlene Condon, MM, saw this when Carla, several weeks after her return, began repeating to Marlene all the painful details of her visit to her mother. She had already told the story at least five times and this time Ita stopped her: "For God's sake, pull yourself up. You don't need to go over that any more...You can't stay there." And Carla agreed that Ita was right. (By now, Carla had nicknamed Ita Ernestina, because she was so earnest and worked so hard.)

In June 1977 there was a major hunger strike in Chile to draw attention to the people who remained disappeared. In December the United Nations condemned the Chilean regime for its continued violation of human rights.

That year Ita sent Maryknoll her reflection on the essence of their mission service:

In many ways Chile is a front line that is a constant challenge to a Christian....Various programs have been created to meet needs—children's dining rooms, health programs, cooperatives, cottage industries, legal help, programs for the families of political and disappeared prisoners. Yet...they are temporary measures that don't touch the source of the problem. At best they serve as a means of denouncing a situation of sin and injustice as well as having the people affected group together in solidarity.

In reflecting about it alone and with others, I see Chile deeply experiencing the paschal mystery, with the light of Easter still to come...The challenge that we live daily is to enter into this mystery with faith. Am I willing to suffer with the people here, the suffering of the powerless, the feeling impotent? *Can I say to my neighbors—I have no solutions to this situation—I don't know the answers, but I will walk with you, search with you, be with you.* Can I let myself be evangelized by this opportunity? Can I look at and accept my own poorness as I learn it from other poor ones?[1] (Author's italics)

Carla sent me a two-page English translation of an article by the Chilean theologian Segundo Galilea, "How the Poor Evangelize Us." It emphasized that the Latin American experience of pastoral renewal had drawn the Church closer to the poor. He wrote: "The poor remind us of the human and suffering face of Jesus, his options and preferences, and that freedom happens by the way of the cross. They keep alive my gospel realism and—I do not know the true Jesus if, in following him, I do not participate in some way in the life of the poor." His words both expressed and reinforced Carla's strong belief in living as, and learning from, the poor.

***

Carla continued to worry about her mother's well-being and her own responsibility. In July she wrote me: "Some days I can put all my trust in the Lord and other days I'm as neurotic as the worst and worry and fret like any nut. It's hard to know for certain—sometimes I think I'm just shirking my duty and then I consider all things and can only opt to continue where I am. Being human and imperfect, I can only trust that if I should take another initiative with mama, it will be indicated. Perhaps it's a help to me to keep alive my commitment to the poor and forgotten here."

In the midst of her despair over the regime's continued repression of the poor, on August 5, 1977, Carla composed a poem she shared with many friends. In "HERE I WILL STAY" she reflected on her renewed commitment to serve in Chile in words that could also express her later commitment to El Salvador:

The Lord has guided me so far

And in His guidance He has up and dropped me here
    at this time and in this place of history.
To search for and find Him.
Not somewhere else.
But here.

And so HERE I WILL STAY,
    until I have found that broken Lord, in all His forms
        and all His various pieces,
    until I have completely bound-up His wounds and
        covered His whole Body, His People
        with the rich oil of gladness.

And when that has been done,
    He will up and drop me again—
Either into His Promised Kingdom, or into the midst
    of another jigsaw puzzle of
His broken Body, His hurting People

Visiting prisoners had become a regular ministry for Carla and Ita. (To pursue her good work, Carla had to borrow a skirt, the required attire for women visiting the men's prison.) La Bandera, like all poblaciones, continued to be treated by the government as a center of active resistance; in many families at least one member had been arrested or disappeared.

The missioners' work, given the tragedies and powerlessness around them, took a tremendous toll. There were no solutions, no progress, and it was dangerous living so close to the fire. And for some months Ita and Carla were the only Maryknoll sisters working in La Bandera, which compounded their burdens.

The unending frustration dragged Carla's spirits down. Ita, too, suffered from stress and frustration. Ita wrote to a friend, "Besides the work—which will never be accomplished, but is a reality we have to live with—and forming a new community, I got involved in group therapy to work on some of my quirks. It was very helpful, even though I can't say I readily volunteered for my times in the frying pan."[2]

On March 3, 1978, Carla wrote "Who Are Chile's Urban Poor?" In it she concluded that many who live under oppression "cannot identify their God in words, but it's seldom that they don't profess his mercy."

That same day Ita sent her own reflection to many friends: "Living with the poor has made me face up to my creatureliness, my impotence in many situations, my own poorness and limitedness and, therefore, having to face (and trying to develop more) the real dependence on the Lord, community and others in my life. Maybe it's been a personal luxury to have come to know and accept myself more among the poor where life is more real and where, possibly, there is less pretense of being other than who one is."[3]

*** *** ***

By August 1977 Ita was due to return to Maryknoll for a year of reflection and renewal before taking her final vows. Such a long absence from mission service seemed unnecessary to her, especially since she was certain of her decision. Not eager to leave, she asked for a year's post-ponement. She was worried that Carla, already in low spir-its and increasingly angered by the government's repression, might get into trouble without her. She had always been the one to pull Carla back, to force her to think things through and not be quite so impulsive. Carla urged Ita to go, insist-ing that she'd be all right. Finally, in April 1978 Ita head-ed to New York. Carla, facing the prospect of a year with-out Ita's strength and support, began visiting Padre Perez at the Benedictine monastery more frequently. "He's a good boy—honest, poor and simple," she wrote to Ita.

On May 22, 1978, a major hunger strike to protest the regime and especially to call attention to the disappeared was held at several Catholic sites in Santiago. The Mary-knoll sisters, along with many other religious, participat-ed. "All we wanted to know was where are the missing?" said Jane Kenrick. The strike continued for more than two weeks, and because the sisters were fasting and drinking only water, they spent much time waiting in long lines for bathrooms. Jane chuckled to recall that Carla's humor kept up their spirits. Carla teased that they should be grateful—after all, waiting in line was much easier and quicker than preparing meals, eating, and cleaning up. "Think of all the time we could save!" she said.[4]

News of the strike made its way to Maryknoll, New York, through the congregation's contacts in Washington, DC. Ita wrote to Connie Pospisil, "Was that ever hard be-ing here! My only urge was to get on a plane and be with you all!" Ita was disappointed—as returned missioners in-variably were—by the lack of news coverage of events in Chile. Her year of reflection included not only intellectu-al and spiritual renewal, but also psychological help to deal with the traumas she had endured in her five years in Chile. The oppression she witnessed had left her exhausted, shak-en, angry, and numb.[5]

While home Ita participated in the sisters' General As-sembly of 1978, which again highlighted their commitment to social justice and a strengthened preferential option for the poor: "The saving mission of the poor is becoming visible to the Church and offering hope to our world. Solidarity with the poor is not an option but a sign of the Kingdom that must be made explicit in our day. We commit ourselves to the cause of the poor through the witness of our lives, our words, and our ministry."[6]

The sisters in La Bandera worked tirelessly to build a faith community in the población. On September 25, 1978, Carla sent a long letter to Betty and Jack to describe a special liturgy:

> Yesterday we had the first celebration in the little chapel that the people here have constructed. Next to your beautiful Church it looks like a shack, but to me it's a sacrament of the effort of these people and their lives. Since we have no priest, I sort of directed the celebration. Instead of everyone saying, "Lord have mercy" one of the ladies made up a prayer asking pardon for all the ills that affect us—the hunger, the violence, the oppression, etc. Then instead of the Gloria, all the people said what they praised God for and we all sung "We praise you, O Lord." The Gospel was read by one of the people and everyone commented on what it meant in real life. Instead of just saying the creed, one of the women said what she believed in and why, which was very powerful since her life, her husband and her kids have really changed since she's come to know the Lord. In fact she even got married after living eleven years with her husband. Then for the offertory I had asked each family to bring a piece of bread. We all thought about what our commitment to one another is—and then the man of the family broke the bread and gave it to his family and to anyone who hadn't brought bread. I went around with a basket and each one as they dropped their piece of bread in said what their commitment was that week. The men said, "I commit myself to work for the daily bread of my family"—or "I commit myself to be a

better father to my children" or "I commit myself to continue working on the chapel" etc. The women committed themselves also to their families, some to working in the dining room for the undernourished kids, and the kids committed themselves to their studies, etc. Instead of communion I asked the men then to give out the bread that was a sign of our commitment to one another as Christ gave himself for us. It was impressive indeed to hear the ole beat-up men saying as they gave out the bread, "This is the bread of my commitment and yours." All in all, I believe that the Lord was praised and known a bit better by the participation of his humble people.

Carla's letter again complained that she missed news from home and was disappointed that her regular letters were not answered: "I'll not ask anymore. Know you are remembered in my prayers and that I care about you both."

In November 1978 Betty traveled alone from Florida to Santiago to see Carla. She was not an experienced or confident traveler. She knew no Spanish. Still, she made the trip. She was terrified when she was detained for a while at the airport because of complications with her paperwork, and the sight of armed men on the streets in Santiago added to her fear. Carla stayed at her side every minute. Although she never ceased loving Carla and treasuring her memory, the trauma of that visit later deterred Betty from visiting Carla's grave in El Salvador.

What drew Betty to Chile during such a dangerous time was that "I missed her so much, and we had things we needed to talk over."[7] It's likely that Betty visited to reassure Carla of their mother's need for a nursing home. Carla saw families in Chile take care of their elderly members at home and may have found the decision to put her mother in an institution difficult to accept. Within months, however, Carla was able to write about her mother, "I thank God she's taken care of and I guess the whole situation is a big test to what my faith is about."

After this visit Carla wrote good-humoredly to Betty: "Everyone asks for you—you made a real impression on all—I guess because as everyone says, you're so gentle and roll with everything. Probably because I'm so wicked and mean you were a welcome relief!" Many members of the Piette family fondly remember Betty as a woman with "a heart as big as the world."

***

The Chilean regime had long shown a frightening capacity for murder beyond its borders. On September 21, 1976, two weeks after Chile revoked his citizenship, Orlando Letelier, who had once been Allende's defense minister and was a vocal opponent of Pinochet, was assassinated, along with his American aide, by a car bomb in Washington, DC. The regime targeted other opponents as well: Bernardo Leighton and his wife escaped a similar attempt in Rome; General Carlos Pratt and his wife were killed by a car bomb in Argentina. In late 1978, the Maryknoll community learned that General Anastasio Somoza's Nicaraguan government had an equally long reach.

In Nicaragua, the Somoza family dynasty, backed by the United States, had ruled since 1936, always supporting the interests of the wealthy oligarchy over those of the poor. In the 1970s members of the religious community, including Maryknoll missioners, were freshly inspired by the preferential option for the poor declared by the Medellín conference of Latin American bishops in 1968.

The regime labeled the missioners—and anyone working for justice, democracy, and social progress for the poor—Communist subversives, thereby justifying violent reprisals against any efforts at social reform. By 1975 General Somoza declared a state of siege and introduced martial law. Censorship, threats of torture and death, and increased violence by the National Guard followed.

In 1978 a prominent opposition leader and newspaper editor, Pedro Joaquin Chamorro, was assassinated. Fifty thousand mourners marched in his funeral procession, which attracted international attention and further unified opposition forces. International human rights groups and the Nicaraguan Catholic bishops condemned the dictatorship. Maura Clarke, MM, on assignment in the States after years of service in Nicaragua, spoke at public protests to call attention to the needs of the suffering Nicaraguan people.

Also in 1978, Estelle Coupe, before traveling from Nicaragua to the United States to attend Maryknoll's general assembly, revisited Chile. She had been Carla's superior in 1964, the one who reprimanded her for her informal manner of addressing the bishop. During Estelle's visit, she and Carla spent time together, and Estelle wept over how violent and brutal life in Chile had become.

Estelle and Peg Dillon, MM, carried to the general assembly a message from Bishop Manuel Salazar Espinoza, the president of the Nicaraguan Conference of Bishops: "Tell the people of the United States that we are fighting for freedom and ask them to support us with a hands-off policy."

While she was home, Estelle gave radio and print interviews in which she spoke candidly about the situation in Nicaragua. Although she requested that these not be broadcast or published until her safe return to Nicaragua, they were made public two weeks before she left the United States. As she and Pat Nolan, MM, drove down a four-lane highway in Mexico on the first day of their return trip, their car was run off the road. Pat later had no memory of the incident, but in the hospital she was heard saying, "Be careful, Estelle, they're trying to push us off the road!" Estelle never regained consciousness and was eventually moved to the congregation's nursing home at Maryknoll, New York.[8]

Carla was devastated when she learned what had happened to Estelle; her grief and anger drove her deeper into depression.

Just a few days after hearing about the accident, despite—or perhaps because of—her grief over Chile's continued oppression of the poor and over Estelle's fate, Carla traveled to a Bolivian Regional Assembly of sisters. She wrote to the sisters in Chile, "Greetings from the top of the world with thin air but colorful groundings....It is refreshing to see new colors, new people and new cultures. I hope I can be open to all the newness and color. I hope you had a jolly new year's feast." Dominican sister Pat De Marco met Carla at the assembly and vividly remembered her quick humor. When sisters passed around a pair of reading glasses to share at the assembly Carla quipped, "I'm glad to see that the sisters in Bolivia also have a common vision!"[9]

That Christmas my mother and I visited Mrs. Piette at St. Paul's Home near Appleton. I wrote Carla to reassure her that her mother, although confused, looked well, was in good spirits, and was pleased to have visitors.

Carla replied: "It really touched me to read of your visit to my Mom. In fact I cried on the bus home from the post office—and that's something for me. However, as you say, which was good for me to hear, God does provide. Another beautiful example of His mercy is that since Mama's been in St. Paul's—at least once a month or every two months I receive some word of her—and never from the [immediate] family. [Sr. Catherine Verbeten, her mother's cousin, who lived close to the nursing home, visited Mrs. Piette and wrote regularly to Carla.] The whole experience of being so far away and trusting Him—I believe helps me here with this inhuman poverty where we live. There is a hard core of strength and goodness that arises from the poor."

She wrote to Betty, "I had a good rest after a summer of meetings and workshops. Now I'm back in the población and must get down to the reality again. I was very happy to hear news of mama and also that she's got friends there. Little by little I believe more and more that the Lord's ways certainly aren't our ways, but that He manifests His love for us in the circumstances of our life the way it is."

***

Carla looked forward to Ita's scheduled return in May 1979, but Ita's plans were unexpectedly derailed. On the eve of her departure for Chile, she was badly injured in a car accident. She was hospitalized for a month with a broken pelvis and torn knee and her return was delayed six months.

Connie Pospisil and Carla were already interested in going to Nicaragua to give the sisters there, who were living through that undeclared war, a rest, and Carla became especially eager to move on after the disappointment of Ita's delayed return. Perhaps she was also motivated because she knew that Estelle, who had been serving in Nicaragua, was still in a coma and might never recover. The Maryknoll regional governing board approved transfers for Connie and Carla, but in spite of their diligent efforts the two sisters could not get into Nicaragua. The continuing conflict had cut off outside communication and the borders were closed. On July 15 Carla wrote to Melinda Roper, MM, president of the Maryknoll sisters, to reaffirm her interest: "If I can be of help I will gladly go for three months or six months or one year. We had a good two day meeting on the Puebla Documents—just getting together was a jolly break in the winter skies."[10]

Two days later, on July 17, 1979, Somoza left Nicaragua in defeat. The long ordeal of insurrection and repression left 50,000 dead and more than half a million homeless. Under new Sandinista leadership, Nicaragua began reconstruction and the implementation of reforms, including literacy programs, throughout the country.

Also in the summer of 1979, Archbishop Oscar Romero in nearby El Salvador issued a plea for experienced Spanish-speaking missioners to join him in working for and with his country's poor. In response, a call went out from Maryknoll for sisters to serve on loan in Central America, especially Nicaragua or El Salvador.

Carla was determined to leave La Bandera and eager to move on. As at other times in her mission life, she felt she had given all she could, that she was drained. Connie Pospisil said that Carla's spirits were dimming and that she desperately clung to her Bible "as she felt her faith slipping out from under her feet. She felt there was too much evil here and she didn't believe that good would triumph over evil."

In La Bandera the bishop's driver overheard the bishop say that Carla had notified him of her intended departure. The driver spread the word to Miguel Cruz and other residents. Miguel recalled that the people of Bandera tried to persuade Carla to stay, but she was adamant. She had made her decision.[11]

In September 1979 Carla wrote to Betty:

> Thank you for the check and card. I know your generosity is sincere and I appreciate what you send but I confess that I prefer a million times a few words about yourself and how you're doing rather than all the Hallmark Cards or checks in the world. Especially now since Jack has been sick and you've been thru a lot. I have one more month of work in Bandera and then I'll be heading down south until the end of the year. Hopefully at the end of the year I may be taking on a new challenge but I'll keep you posted.

> I have come to see…that what I have most feared has really taught me the most. How I've wished that I could be with you during this time. Since I can't, I send you my prayers and my desire for Jack's health and for both of you the Lord's peace that comes after such struggles.

Carla sent Betty a gift—a semi-precious stone from Chile called the Cross Stone. "Since you've known in many circumstances of your life that the Cross is very present and especially lately [Jack was seriously ill], I send you this as something beautiful even though it is the Cross."

Carla wrote many friends about the energy and enthusiasm she felt at the prospect of a new assignment. "Leaving Chile takes its toll," she wrote to Fr. Ganss. "However, I'm experiencing a freedom like wings, picking up the torn up roots and a real peace."

To Crowbar she wrote:

> In spite of the fact that I turned 40 this year I feel younger and ready to accept a new challenge. So I

volunteered for Central America, which may be either El Salvador or Nicaragua. I've been in Chile now for almost 16 years and before I enter into my dotage (which I pray may never happen) I want to be able to give of my gifts and self where I'm needed and where I can learn to be and care for others.

The news I get from home is always very scarce but apparently my mother is adapting a bit better at St. Paul's Home. I thank God that she is there and I must admit, Crowbar, that all the resentment and feeling I had towards her are going away. I can say it has been a long road of healing and falling into the same bad habits and getting up again with the help of the Lord and in the work that I do—of listening to others' problems—I believe it teaches a lot.

CHAPTER SEVEN

Coelemu

IN THE FALL OF 1979 Becky Quinn, Carla's friend from her early years in Chillán, was working alone in Coelemu, a small settlement in the countryside far south of Santiago. Knowing that Carla desperately needed a change, Becky invited Carla to join her while they awaited word about a possible assignment in Nicaragua and Ita's eventual return.

In October Carla gave away almost everything she owned, packed her few remaining possessions in a small shopping bag, and moved to Coelemu. "The Lord is calling me to be poor with his poor," she said once more. Her desire to move to Central America, another place where she could live and eat as poorly as the poorest and own nothing, was to her "a new thing." (Her favorite Biblical passage, Isaias 43, reads in part: "Fear not, for I have redeemed thee. Behold, I do new things. I will make a way in the wilderness, and rivers in the desert.")

In mid-November she wrote to Grandma Ford, by now her good friend and adopted mother, that Coelemu and its rolling hills lifted her drooping spirits. She admitted that Bandera was "getting to me," that she was finding peace and happiness in this new environment, and that she was still eagerly looking forward to moving north to a new mission.

Carla often said that she had died in Bandera, that she was "spent out." Laura Magellanes, MM, described Carla's burnout in Bandera and her rebirth in Coelemu:

La Bandera was a tough place...oppressive, very poor. People with hard lives, deprived, more aggressive. I think her time was up in that población. She had been there a long time and under the tensions of the población, the military, the takeover, the comedor, the fights you'd have...the poverty of the people, trying to convince others to help those poor people, the whole strain of it.

The Carla that came back from Coelemu was OLD TIME CARLA. She had no pressures upon her, she was free again, it was the old Carla, the creative Carla, the happy Carla, because the campo [country] life and being with Rebecca who is an organizer and real good person, got things going. It was Becky's easygoing manner and her terrific sense of humor and acceptance of the other person. That campo life, very warm people in Coelemu just released all the tightness in her.

Several other sisters have also described Carla's experience in Coelemu as a resurrection, a rebirth. Becky, who lived with her during those months, wrote:

Those last two months in Chile were the happiest for herself and most memorable for me. We prayed daily, shared our joys and experiences and felt more "community" than when surrounded by others. Carla— a loyal friend, a joyous generous giver, an extremely creative person—was so well-accepted here. She just blossomed. Gone were her phobias on so many issues...healed by the kindness of the people, the greenness of the campo, the responses of her call to Mission.

Carla suffered much because she was so sensitive to life and it was here that the Lord chose to have her "healing." She herself claimed she was healed of many prejudices during her stay in Coelemu. The last few weeks were phenomenal—she would just desire something and it would happen. I told her to be careful what she expressed to God because it seemed they were in direct and immediate communication.

An example happened in Chillán while visiting there to say good-bye to old friends. She had an ex-alumno [student] she'd not seen in 7 years—when she was a teacher there he had gone to Argentina and we went to a store where she'd got him a part time job years ago. They said he was coming soon for a visit but had not seen him. Within the half-hour she left me to do another job and then bumped into him by the gas station! They sat down and visited for awhile. [This was Mariano, the boy she'd brought into her second grade class when he was fourteen.] Carla felt leaving Chile was hard, but made easier when she met some other ex-alumnas that were entering religion, she felt her work continuing in them. Three of her girl students from San Vicente School in Chillan entered religious life and attributed their vocations to Carla.

It surprised Carla she could be so happy here—with her work, her relationships, her community, and herself.

In Coelemu she was so happy and content that she might have stayed, had she not already decided on Central America. To Betty and Jack she wrote:

When you hold onto things that make you happy they have the tendency to fade and crumble. So many times in my life I have had to give up something very precious only to be gifted with something else I never dreamed of asking for, but received in my poorness with great gratitude and lately with joy. When I left La Bandera I was quite dead in many ways. I went to the south to work in a mission where I didn't even have a room but rather slept in the hall, and since the other Sister and I were only renting a room we had to eat with the priests, which I can't say I enjoy.

However, I came to love the work so much that even
the priests weren't hard to take and by the time I left
I enjoyed them as good brothers with whom I could
joke and fight and really learn from.

Carla bought scraps of pastel material and asked a neighbor to make her a dress as a symbol of the new life she
was experiencing in Coelemu. The dress was three or four
shades of green—the color of life—with specks of yellow
and brown. She called it her resurrection or rainbow dress.
It was also her only dress.

***

In November 1979, before she returned to Chile, Ita visited the Maryknoll sisters in Nicaragua. Although she was
strongly considering a move to Central America, her decision was not yet final. After a brief stay in Santiago, she
boarded a train south for Coelemu. Carla met her at the station, wearing a t-shirt painted with butterflies and "Welcome home, Ita." (The paints were washable and Carla frequently painted a fresh message for a new occasion.)

That year Carla sent Christmas cards printed with the final stanzas of the poem, "Dark Earth Still Needs Your Star,"
that she had written soon after the 1973 coup. She thanked
Grandma Ford for encouraging the Maryknoll priest who
arranged their printing. In notes to Fr. Ganss, her relatives,
and friends she shared her excitement about her new move:
"The move northward—as I take another step in the circus
of life—will be another root pull but I'm happy to be able
to go. I trust that the Lord of mission leads with sure steps."
At this point she was headed first for Nicaragua, undecid-
ed whether she would ultimately serve in Nicaragua or El
Salvador.

In January 1980 the Maryknoll sisters in Chile, including Carla and Ita, held a discernment retreat facilitated by
David Ratermann, an archdiocesan priest from St. Louis
and a brother of Joan Ratermann. The sisters meditated for

several days on the beatitudes and suffering in the context of the possible call to El Salvador and Nicaragua. Several sisters expressed concern for the dangers and demands that Carla and Ita might face in either country, especially because Ita had only recently regained physical health and Carla's mental health had been so fragile. But Carla remained determined to serve in Central America.[1]

On January 11, 1980, Ita wrote her mother, "There have been some lovely testimonies to Carla for her 15 years in Chile—especially from one of our friends, Eduard Alvear, a Franciscan priest with whom we worked in Bandera. He came this morning and gave a beautiful homily on how Carla had touched his life and priesthood."

A Chilean parish where Carla had helped out gave her a small gold medal as a good-bye gift. In honor of her clown spirit the front of the medal bore the face of a clown; the back was inscribed, "Hma Carla, Los Hermanos, Pquia San Francisco, Chile." On her way to Nicaragua Carla sent the medal to Crowbar. "You've been a good friend," she wrote, "and I never really have anything to give you—so I'd like you to have this. I'm not the great jewelry wearer, you know, and I can assure you—you'll never receive another one." Karen was deeply touched—and also amused that Carla considered the medal jewelry.[2]

Before leaving Chile, Carla visited her spiritual advisor, Padre Pedro Perez, at the Benedictine monastery. When she first told him that she wished to go to Central America, he was concerned because she seemed very tired and he advised her to reconsider. "It was impossible, she was very firm about her ideas and plans," he later said. "Although we spoke about this idea several times, she never wavered. And so I ended up saying a prayer to send her to mission... and invoked the Spirit of Jesus that he would accompany her wherever she was called to go."

After Carla's death, Padre Perez wrote to Maryknoll, "It is not often that I have known a person as restless and admiring of Jesus as Carla. This called my attention very strongly. A simple woman, with humor, conflictive in matters of justice and humble. Yes, humble before God and her own life, from deep inside."

On January 14 Carla set off for Nicaragua, wearing her rainbow dress, carrying her one small bag, and saying, as always, "Do I need more?"

She wrote frequently to Becky and Betty during her travels through Peru and Panama. From Lima, to Becky: "Very good to be here...gives my heart time to weep and recover. I've been making many rainbows so far with tears of joy. But I'm glad I'm a Pilgrim again."

To her sister: "Many times I've been as the beggar, giving one little kernel. Now, when I left Chile, I can truly say I've given all that I knew at the time—friends, work, even culture and the history of a people I had grown to love and appreciate and yet I believe that Our Father is so generous and loving—He'll do even more and be more in Nicaragua or Salvador—wherever I end up."

While in Panama she wrote Becky: "My praying habits are changing as I've come to favor the nighttime since it's cooler and the stars link me to the past. Also night is quite sacramental insofar as it's still unknown where I'll hang up my clown. The Father has been very generous and I've been able to hang loose. I get attacks of nostalgia but it's good to mourn when one has had a heart of stone for so long. The heat here is delightful—in fact I believe it might make me warmer in a deeper way. Will I ever be able to be less than a poor pilgrim in that area, Becky? I guess it's what the dueño del circo [circus master] wants at this time so that He can better direct the whole show."

In Nicaragua, just six months after that country's liberation, Carla joined Maryknoll sisters Joan Uhlen and Jean Roberts at Ocatal. She plunged in immediately to make home visits, with special attention to the sick, the elderly, and the outcast. Joan recalled Carla's artistic spirit, her dedication to the poor and suffering people, and her ability to quickly bond with them.[3]

Carla wrote Becky that Ocatal reminded her of Coelemu:

> The dear poor are very present as I begin to visit in order to be doing something as I await how the Lord of complicated cases and surprises will arrange Salvador. This city is ten times poorer than Coelemu. One of the little things one forgets about war is that most things are "removed." The houses are "elado" [crushed] and the people are so thin I feel like the fat lady of the circus, although I've lost about five pounds.

> I'm very happy here even tho I'm still hanging in not knowing where this Pilgrim will hang up her clown—reading a very interesting book called *Your Erroneous Zones* by Dr Wayne Dyer. It's very positive and helps me a lot. The Lord I find here is a joyful Lord—a very poor, simple, smiling-eyed Lord and aware that the liberation continues. Days ago I had a big thrill—I shook Daniel Ortega's hand—one of the members of the junta and one of the faithful freedom fighters. I never thought I'd get excited about such things but—even I have changed. The guys are so simple and friendly.

Carla was horrified at the physical devastation—the shattered and leveled buildings—caused by the war and at the human devastation—the tortures and killings—committed by the National Guard. She was impressed by the spirit of the people and the excitement of beginning alfabetización (literacy) programs, which had formerly been forbidden. "The new vocabulary here is Liberation, ... but it's been a long hard road. It's gorgeously warm at all times! Bananas are coming out of my ears and watermelons blowing me up, but I waddle down the road like all of us beat-up pilgrims, trying to live one day at a time."

Saying "I'm in the looking around stage," Carla visited El Salvador for two weeks in February. To get there, she had to travel through Honduras, which had been at odds with El Salvador since 1969. Entering El Salvador could be dangerous for several reasons: the stand-off between Honduras and El Salvador; the Salvadoran government's fear of revolutionaries entering from Nicaragua after the overthrow of Somoza's regime; and the escalating violence in El Salvador itself between security forces and the growing number of protestors. In addition, guerillas in El Salvador sometimes burned buses to cause disruptions.

El Salvador was a wrenching contrast to newly liberated Nicaragua. Fear and distrust were everywhere and mutilated bodies dumped on the roadsides were common sights. Carla was profoundly inspired by Archbishop Romero and the opportunity to work with him. She admired his "great holiness and love for the truth." To Betty she wrote, "Still I like this place with its spunky people—it's a concentrated little bouillon cube of a country."

On February 20, while waiting to hear Ita's decision, Carla sent Ita her "Reflections on El Salvador," which appears to confirm her decision to move there. "This says where I am in front of the Father who has this whole thing in His hands," she wrote:

On a walk

  Thru the ugly town

    It is evident

      That immaculate Mr. Affluent

        Has passed thru

        Leaving his campaign kiss upon all.

Our God is present in your powerlessness,

  Dear little people.

    Do you see him with you?

      Do you realize that your ways

        Are the ways of His Kingdom?

Does the smell of wet kindling
   Soaked by lies, violence, injustice and idolatry
   Make you sick enough to search for
   Other sticks, and burn other wood?

I want to join you,
   Little people.
      Please let me into your game.
      Can I await the dawn with you?
      I am poor, too.

During this period of preparation for her new assignment, Carla wrote "Attitudes Necessary for Pastoral Work," in which she emphasized the importance of listening—especially to the poor—of questioning, and of prayer: "There is no manual other than that of the Gospel as to how to proceed in pastoral work....There are many professors in our daily searching, but the essential thing is to know how to listen to them. We ought [to] listen to the people—especially the poor, the sinners, those who live lives farthest from the values of the world....To have an attitude of a sinner (truly and not pretending)...saves the pastoral agent from false pride and directs the work toward the weak, the fallen."

She saw an attitude of poverty as essential: "(1) as far as material goods go in order to identify ourselves with the dispossessed; (2) as far as teaching materials so that we are...not using yesterday's materials for today's challenges,...and (3) as far as our own being, so that we really need a Saviour." She emphasized, "We should travel lightly of baggage and be confident that Pentecost will come when we need it—neither early nor late."

And, always, an attitude of prayerfulness: "A worker cannot work well without eating well; a pastoral agent cannot work well without praying."

In "Some Observations on Urban Pastoral Work," which she wrote around the same time, Carla noted: "To the extent that we walk with the people, reflect with them and with other pastoral agents, and dialogue with the Master, we will see that the communion of redeemed sinners, or of those on the road to liberation, is as strong as the communion of saints."

She concluded by urging missioners not to be afraid to share personally: "How many times I have heard someone say: 'She never gave or shared anything of herself—I didn't know her.' If we are happy, let us share the happiness; if we are discouraged, let us share our disillusionment. At times the most necessary and difficult lesson to learn is how to receive affection or support—or simply friendship."

On March 3, 1980, Fr. Cesar Jerez, SJ, the Jesuit provincial for Central America, visited the Jesuits of the parish of Ocotal. The Maryknoll Sisters asked him to discuss the situation in El Salvador and whether it was better to remain in Nicaragua or go to El Salvador. He met Carla, who asked him, "What would give greater glory to God? To go to El Salvador or remain in Nicaragua?" He appreciated the way she presented her question in Ignatian style and replied in favor of El Salvador, which reinforced her decision. Later Fr. Jerez said, "I admired Carla and Ita's dedication, their simplicity and their commitment, the one rather large like the strong woman in the Gospel, the other fragile, like a reed in the desert." They asked him to be their regular spiritual advisor; he teased them that such pious women did not need him. They insisted, and he did agree to "accompany them" when he could, usually at 7 a.m. meetings.

On March 17, during a St. Patrick's Day party, Ita called from Chile to announce that she had decided for El Salvador and that she planned to arrive in Nicaragua in April.

Carla wrote Becky about feeling homesick for Chile—the people and her friends. "However, I keep asking Our Father to help me live in the present—so fully and deeply that only the present is here and He has heard my prayer. Now I have trouble at times with the future. Yesterday I saw a rainbow here, which was most consoling."

She wrote to the sisters in Chile, "Being Carla, I have days when I'm good at being a pilgrim cooking Chilean dishes and jollying up the girls—and then I have days when being a pilgrim is a drag on myself and the other clowns. However, the Lord of the circus has been very generous and I believe will continue to direct the show and the daily performance will go on. I remember you all in my prayer and my nightly dreams don't let me forget either Chile—its beautiful scenery—or people."

"Every day of my pilgrimage since I left Chile has been one of learning and receiving," Carla wrote, "learning in the university of listening to little people, in the lecture hall of pastoral agents analyzing their realities. I won't come out with a title or degree, but a more valuable education could not be achieved anywhere."[4]

She again planned to take a bus to El Salvador, despite the possible dangers. She hoped to return to Nicaragua to join Maryknoll sisters in León for a workshop during Easter week and then "dolly back to Savior land" with Ita.

CHAPTER EIGHT

El Salvador

EL SALVADOR, a tiny country the size of Massachusetts and the smallest in Central America, lies wedged between Honduras and Guatemala. In 1980 its population of five million was the densest in Central America. Military dictators, supported by the "14 Families" of wealthy landowners, had ruled the country since 1944. In earlier times, many peasant families, the *campesinos*, were able to survive on their small harvests. However, as wealthy landowners enlarged their holdings to increase their sugar cane and coffee crops, more and more of the rural poor had to struggle for survival. In the 1960s several political parties initiated a movement toward centrist democracy that included a push for workers' unions and agrarian reform. Government repression soon followed. During that time the military government, wealthy families, and U.S. government agents established ORDEN (Organizacion Democrática Nacionalista), a paramilitary death squad of mercenaries whose job was to crack down on rural unrest through brutal violence. In following years the CIA continued to provide guidance and training to Salvadoran intelligence and security personnel.[1]

In 1972 and 1976 the moderate reform parties were defeated in presidential elections dominated by widespread fraud. The military regime remained in power, and reformers, concluding that progress was not possible under such corrupt and repressive governments, initiated protests, strikes, and other direct actions against the government. After 1975 the regime escalated the level of violence,

109

repression, and atrocities. It publicly depicted all advocates of reform—whether human rights activists, union organizers, strikers, campesinos, students, or religious workers who sided with the poor—as subversive, dangerous Marxists. The military, National Guard, police, and death squads were free to kill or disappear anyone thought to be working for—or merely sympathetic with—reform. Members of the religious community were particularly suspect, but poor campesinos were the most frequent victims. Some wealthy landowners contracted for National Guard or ORDEN squads to protect their property.

In February 1977 Oscar Romero was named to the prominent post of archbishop of San Salvador. A native Salvadoran, Romero had grown up in the hills near the Honduran border. As a pastor he had witnessed the worsening poverty of the campesinos, the injustices they suffered, and the violence they endured at the hands of the National Guard. They lacked adequate food, health care, and shelter; many plantation workers were treated as slaves and forced to sleep on the cold, damp ground.

On February 28, 1977, shortly after Romero's installation as archbishop, government forces fired on crowds peacefully protesting election fraud. Just days later, on March 12, Romero's close friend Rutilio Grande, SJ, along with a young boy and an elderly man, was ambushed and slaughtered by a death squad. Grande, a dedicated pastor, had worked for years with the poor sugar cane workers in rural Aguilares. His murder was clearly seen as a penalty for organizing the workers.

Romero reacted vigorously. First, joined by one hundred priests, he concelebrated a funeral Mass for Grande at the cathedral. He declared, "The government should not consider a priest who takes a stand for social justice as a politician, or a subversive element, when he is fulfilling his mission in the politics of the common good."[2]

Next, Romero announced that in all of El Salvador on the following Sunday there would be only one "single Mass" and that he would cancel all other Masses. He celebrated the single Mass on the steps of the cathedral before a crowd of 100,000.

And, finally, Romero publicly demanded a government investigation of Grande's murder. Without one, he said, archdiocesan representatives would no longer appear with members of the government at official ceremonies. The government took no action and Romero refused to attend the inauguration of the country's new president in July 1977.

Romero made these decisions after consultation with and agreement from his diocesan priests. However, most Salvadoran bishops strongly disagreed with his actions and they denounced him to Rome. Concerned that the Pope understand the context within which he had acted, Romero traveled to Rome in late March to meet with Pope Paul VI. After Romero presented documentation of events in El Salvador, the Pope offered his encouragement. "Courage!" the Pope urged. "You are the one in charge!"[3]

After his return, Archbishop Romero established a permanent archdiocesan Justice and Peace Commission to discover and document the truth about human rights abuses, including killings, torture, and disappearances. Each week he included its report—a listing of that week's dead, arrested, and disappeared—in his Sunday homily, which was broadcast throughout the country by archdiocesan radio.

The government publicly accused clergymen who worked with the poor of being "bad priests"; from 1977 to 1979 government forces murdered several more. In January 1979 the National Guard gunned down Fr. Octavio Ortiz and four youths at a church retreat. The regime viewed the Jesuits as the most dangerous priests and warned them to leave the country or face death. Posted handbills urged: "Be a Patriot—Kill a Priest."

In 1977 a diocesan priest, shortly before he was expelled from El Salvador after two years of service, wrote of his work with base Christian communities: "I believe that liberation theology on the parish level is in the making of our own tired section of San Salvador, when our group leaders meet in my living room every Thursday: two nuns, a street peddler, a store clerk, a construction worker or two, a housewife or two, a gas station attendant, a day laborer often without work, my landlady. We pray, we sing, we study, we plan, we evaluate, we laugh and we read revelation to maintain hope. Outside the door there might be a street fight, since we live in one of the skid rows of the city; around the corner people live in cardboard shacks. The 'ears' of the security forces are everywhere, as are the unemployed, the shoeless kids. And the shoeless adults."[4]

In June 1978 Archbishop Romero traveled again to Rome and once again was encouraged by Pope Paul VI. The pope understood the challenge of the archbishop's work and how it could be misunderstood. He reiterated support for the people who were seeking their rights and, as Romero wrote, "spoke words of encouragement and understanding and made me the messenger of his great pastoral affection for our people."[5]

In May 1979 the blatant violence in El Salvador finally became visible to the rest of the world. During a protest at the cathedral, called because five noted reform leaders had been arrested and were missing, government troops again fired on a peaceful crowd, leaving 25 dead and 70 wounded. International television cameras recorded the scene and the film was shown worldwide. Government forces killed 123 unarmed civilians that May.[6]

It was at this time in El Salvador's history, the summer of 1979, that Romero issued his appeal for experienced missioners to accompany his people, the poor. The Cleveland mission team had been active in La Libertad, El Salvador, for many years. By August 1979, the team included Dorothy Kazel, OSU, and Christine Rody, VSC, lay missioner Jean Donovan, and diocesan priests Paul Schindler and Ken Myers. In addition, Maryknoll sister Madeline (Maddie) Dorsey, who had arrived in 1975, ran a health clinic in Colonia Lamatapec, a slum community of four thousand in the city of Santa Ana. Joan Petrik, MM, a more recent arrival, ran a small rural parish nearby, which Paul Schindler tried to visit regularly in order to offer Mass.

As conditions grew worse, the missioners struggled to help refugee families with their emergency needs, particularly by distributing food and first aid supplies and providing health care. That August Dorothy wrote to a friend that another priest had been killed in his church and that their mission team was busy trying to identify and bury, or burn, rotting bodies that had been dumped along the roads. By October the Cleveland team was seriously considering leaving the country. But because they did not want to abandon the people, they chose to stay.[7]

In October 1979 a reformist junta overturned the government and promised to end right-wing terrorism and to continue advancing agrarian reforms. However, repression, murders, and atrocities continued to escalate; there were no reforms. In January 1980 several members of the new government resigned in protest. In response to a large public protest in San Salvador government forces killed twenty demonstrators and wounded two hundred. In his weekly homily, Romero grieved and honored those who had shed their blood while demonstrating peacefully for justice.

As in Chile, agrarian reform was critical to help peasants who lacked any piece of land to feed their families. The Church had supported the growth of farmers unions and land reform as key to the dignity of each person. Although in the mid-1970s modest land reform laws had been passed, they were often opposed by the ruling class. The United States worked through Alliance for Progress in El Salvador to encourage the reforms.

Although subsequent juntas promised sweeping changes when they took power, each continued to declare a state of siege. Tensions increased and the murder of activists grew more common. The worsening situation in the spring of 1980 led to a broad coalition of many civic organizations, both urban and rural, called the Frente Democrático Revolucionario.[8] It is estimated that one-third of the campesinos joined the insurgency.

In February 1980 Romero appealed to U.S. President Jimmy Carter to stop sending U.S. military aid to the junta;

he emphasized to Carter that the current government was even more repressive than the previous one. Before sending the letter, he read it to the congregation during his Sunday homily and received their strong support.

President Carter rejected the appeal. The U.S. continued its military aid.[9] By late February Romero had established a refugee center stocked with food and medical supplies on the seminary grounds in San Salvador, in case of all-out civil war. By March, when Carla moved to El Salvador, at least 3,500 peasants had sought refuge at the center. Most had fled their villages after seeing their homes and crops burned and members of their families killed.

The Maryknoll sisters who volunteered for El Salvador in response to Romero's invitation to accompany his suffering people were to some extent aware of the violence in the country, but they were not at all prepared for the atrocities and extreme hostility toward the church.

The sisters stepped into what became an undeclared civil war, a war of extermination against a civilian population, a government persecution of the Church. It was unparalleled institutionalized violence. "Living is the exception and dying the rule," stated the Salvadoran Human Rights Commission in February 1980.[10] This was not a civil war between two armed and roughly equal groups but rather an extended rebellion against the violence perpetrated by the government's forces and death squads against civilians.

When the war finally ended in 1993 through UN-sponsored peace accords, more than 75,000 unarmed civilians had been murdered and 8,000 more disappeared. "In examining the staggering breadth of the violence that occurred in El Salvador, the [UN Truth] Commission was moved by the senselessness of the killings, the brutality with which they were committed, the terror they created in the people, in other words, the madness, or *locura*, of the war."[11]

In his pastoral letters and homilies Archbishop Romero repeatedly spoke out against the violence. On March 16, 1980, his two-hour homily focused on reconciliation. He called on all sides to abandon violence. To the armed guerilla groups he said, "To those who advocate violent solutions, I appeal to understand that nothing violent can be lasting. There are still prospects, even human ones, for reasonable solutions. And above all there is God's word, which has cried to us today: reconciliation! God wills it—let us be reconciled."[12]

On Sunday March 23, 1980, Romero's homily was, as usual, disseminated widely on loudspeakers outside the cathedral and on radio broadcasts throughout the country. He again appealed forcefully to all sides for an end to the violence. He pleaded with the Salvadoran soldiers and police to stop attacking their fellow Salvadorans, urging them to disobey immoral orders to kill: "Brothers, you are part of our own people. You kill your own campesino brothers and sisters…. It is time to recover your consciences." He ended his homily with a final plea: "In the name of God, and in the name of this suffering people whose laments rise to heaven each day more tumultuous, I beg you, I ask you, I order you in the name of God: Stop the repression!"

He was murdered the next day. At 6:25 on the evening of March 24, a sniper's bullet struck the archbishop in the heart as he said Mass in the small, serene chapel on the grounds of the Hospital of Divine Providence where he lived.[13]

That same evening, a few minutes after six, Carla arrived in San Salvador. Maddie Dorsey and Joan Petrik met her bus and drove her in their jeep over the rough roads to Maddie's home in Santa Ana, two or three hours away. When they arrived, grief-stricken villagers told them that just hours earlier Archbishop Romero had been assassinated. However, no radio stations in El Salvador carried the news. The sisters could learn more only from a Nicaraguan station.

Two days later Carla wrote to Regina McEvoy, vice-president of the Maryknoll sisters:

> Here I am sitting on the steps of the cathedral in San Salvador where the body of Archbishop Romero has been brought in silent procession from the Basilica. I

wanted to get off a few lines to you since I recall how Romero moved you as he moved most little people of El Salvador—and apparently moved the powerful to hate him so much as to kill him.

The sadness that slowly settles over a people with the death of a father, pastor, guide and prophet is the sadness that Salvador is now wrapped in. I wanted to share some of the reflections from the sermon of Ricardo Urioste, the Vicar General. How many times, it was recalled, Romero begged, supplicated and repeated, "Do not kill!" It was with banners that repeated that simple statement that the Archbishop's body was marched to the cathedral.

The Archbishop was a man of prayer, of terrific simplicity and the beautiful humility of a gentle, small man who hardly raised his voice in his Sunday sermons. The Vicar General finished his sermon saying, "Of what good are the beautiful highways of our country if they only serve to transport the blood-stained bodies of innocent victims of the violence present here?" Bishop Romero is the seventh priest killed in El Salvador since 1977. One of the Vicars whom I met yesterday said, "It's good you've come since we have no security as to how long we have. If they do this— kill a man as beautiful as Romero—the green wood— what is left for us?"

To Becky Quinn in Chile Carla wrote:

Here I am in the land of my dreams and desires where I believe, as the Lord says in Isaias 43, "I am doing a new thing." I have cried so much since arriving here, I feel I've arrived to cry with the pueblo.

Yesterday I went to the Cathedral for Mass and unworthily was privileged to be in the guard of honor for this saintly man who gave his life for the poor. As I stood before his body I prayed that I may be converted also from my pride and egoism to be of the pueblo, as I watched the masses file by and cry with me. I believe I am being healed. I believe that this country is being healed at the high price of blood and lives. Now I am entering into a new history and I want to follow the Lord of History as He wants.

Today all the buses are on strike in protest of Archbishop Romero's death so I've been riding trucks. It's practically pornographic how we have to hold on to one another since there are no ropes or anything. Yet in it all, the great Circus Master directs the show.

Now I'm into praying for the conversion of the USA since I believe the Lord wants not the death of a sinner but rather that he turn and live. At least we gringos never have to look for something to be sorry about— we belong to a nationality that has committed so many atrocities against little people that I believe we'll always be able to say, "Have mercy on us, Lord, we are sinners!" And yet the craziness is the great love of the Father I feel in all of this—I guess 'cause Jesus loves sinners so much.

I am tired from mourning—not tired of it but tired from it—so I ask the Lord of the beatitudes to open me to the comfort He always sends.

Archbishop Romero's funeral took place on March 30, Palm Sunday. Although church dignitaries from around the world concelebrated his funeral Mass, only one Salvadoran bishop, Arturo Rivera y Damas, chose to be present. At the funeral Archbishop John Quinn of San Francisco, president of the National Conference of Catholic Bishops, reiterated Romero's plea to President Carter to halt U.S. military aid to El Salvador.

Romero's casket was placed on the steps outside the cathedral so that the celebrants could face the crowd of more than 100,000 mourners in the plaza. Many priests, brothers, and sisters, including Carla, Maddie, and Terry Alexander,

MM, newly arrived from Panama, filled the inside of the cathedral.

As representatives of the popular movement approached to lay flower wreaths in honor of Romero, shots were fired into the crowd and small explosions went off. For forty-five minutes, the gunfire and bombs continued. Panic spread. Fleeing people tried to push into the cathedral. Many of the mourners, especially women, the elderly, and children, were trapped against the fence that surrounded the cathedral grounds and were trampled in the rush to escape. Forty died. The injured and dying were carried into the cathedral. Carla had brought a supply of water with her that day and the sisters shared it with the injured. Terry Alexander later said she that knew it would be dangerous when she volunteered for El Salvador. I asked if she was afraid of dying that day. She smiled as she described the horror and bedlam in the cathedral and said, "I didn't think God would let me die so soon, when He just got me here."

Ita was en route to El Salvador when she heard news of the violence at Romero's funeral. She attended a meeting at which bishops who had been present at the funeral issued their statement to contradict and correct the official government version of events. The Salvadoran government blamed insurgents for the gunfire. Bishops and other witnesses disagreed, for they had seen snipers firing into the crowd from the roof of a nearby government building that faced the plaza.

In April, soon after Romero's funeral, the Maryknoll sisters from Nicaragua and El Salvador gathered in León, Nicaragua, to reflect on their role in those countries. They sent a summary of their reflection, with a reaffirmed commitment to El Salvador, to their Maryknoll sisters, families, and friends.

Carla sent me a copy with a handwritten note: "Altho I had a good 2 month experience in Nicaragua I've been in Salvador for all the excitement and will be there. You can share this but please not with the news media—Salvador is very tight and rather violent, needless to say."

The summary recounted the events of Romero's murder and the violence that erupted at his funeral. It also described violence before the funeral: "When his body was transferred from the basilica to the cathedral gunshots from the guardia caused panic in the ranks of the sisters who were leading the procession, but within minutes they were back in line again with a determination that said 'we've got to go on.'" Even during the crush of crowds fleeing gunshots on the plaza and people dying, most people tried to help others.

In the summary, the sisters also described their thoughts during those moments: "I stood in front of the Lord with empty hands." "I felt a real strength from our martyrs. I was aware of a loving Father." "I repeated Isaias 43, 'No harm will come to you, I am with you.'" "Someone said 'and if harm does come, that's alright, too.'" "A sense of helplessness but an experience of peace." "We are not saviors." "Would God bring me here to die?—No, not yet. I am here to accompany the Salvadoran people in their sorrows, sufferings and fears."

Ita and Carla returned to El Salvador the week after the gathering in León and spent days in meetings with other religious personnel to begin defining their assignment. Ita wrote her mother, "All plans here are short range and every day is ad hoc. There are no absolutes."

During the vigil at the basilica before Romero's funeral, Carla's passport and glasses had been stolen, and consequently she had to spend many hours dealing with the bureaucracy of the American Embassy, which she disparaged for its "buzzers, searchers, guards, bars, and gloom." Getting her papers replaced was critically important, so she wrote to my mother, asking her to obtain official copies of her birth certificate: "Greetings from your wandering missioner of old memories! Naturally my nerves are not pristine, but I haven't had the chaos that the history of Nicaragua has imposed on residents." She even remembered to ask how the Hansen golf game was going. She asked my mother to send her two copies, "with all the seals, signatures and ribbons that turn on the Latin American bureaucracy," in separate mailings. Later she learned that the Salvadoran embassy in New York had to authorize the documents first, so when they finally reached her she forwarded them to Mrs. Ford in New York. Delays ensued. The final approved papers did not arrive until September, when Dorothy Kazel brought them on her return to El Salvador.

Carla, Ita, and Terry had come to El Salvador in answer to Romero's urgent call. His death left them—and all who mourned him—reeling and adrift. As missioners, they also felt robbed of the chance to work under his inspiring leadership. Ita wrote of free-floating anxiety and said, "I appreciate that many people will be concerned about us. We're also concerned for each other and will be doing our best to support and care for each other."[14]

Carla wrote to friends, "Pray for us…especially that the sense of humor may NOT turn into a sense of horror." She and Ita planned to stay in Santa Ana with Maddie Dorsey "while the country is so wild" and to advance one day at a time. Nevertheless, she called it a privileged time. Maddie praised Carla's creativity and the depth of her spirituality as she remembered that Easter season they spent together. "Our shared community life and prayer life was very precious—the most precious of my long life in many missions," she said.

Carla and Ita, in addition to coping without Romero, faced other significant challenges. In Chile they had worked with an urban population; they had no experience in a rural setting. In Chile they had the strong support of the church hierarchy and a large community of Maryknoll missioners and other religious. In El Salvador only one bishop, Rivera y Damas, supported Romero's work, and there were few missionary sisters—just five Maryknollers and the Cleveland mission team—and not only were they separated by distance, numerous military checkpoints, and the threats of violence, but their movements were monitored. In Chile they had lived in one place, serving and nurturing one community. In El Salvador they were literally on the road, staying at various times with Maddie in Santa Ana, the Asunción Sisters in San Salvador, the Cleveland team in La Libertad, and at an Asunción convent in Chalatenango.

Carla lived just five months in El Salvador, much of it on the road. The work was exhausting and every journey was complicated by military checkpoints, searches, and the threat of violence. In the five months, she wrote no poems, but she did write "Lord of the Road."[15]

You are the Lord of the road—

of the life and the truth and the light

Lead us today, and at the same time, be for us the way.

Lord that we may see— Lord that we may hear.

Lord that we may love—Lord that we may understand.

Lord that we may pardon— Lord that we may console.

Lord that we may laugh—Lord that we may cry.

Lord that we may be FREE—

Lord that we may be in solidarity

With your poor ones now.

Carla and Ita sang the song as they bounced across the bouillon cube of a country in the beat-up secondhand jeep, which Carla named La Tonquita (Miss Piggy) because it could navigate mudholes "like a pig in a puddle."

Carla and Ita wrote often to friends, family, and fellow sisters. Their words best convey their struggle to find their way and the harshness and brutality faced by the poor. Carla wrote me, "I pray that I not get hardened to the atrocities I experience."

El Salvador was consumed by lawlessness. Government forces massacred whole villages. People could be killed for any reason—or no reason at all. Mutilated bodies were routinely dumped on city streets and country roads. Because of the violence directed toward anyone in the Catholic Church who served the poor and the victims of violence, it was no longer possible for missionaries to do pastoral work with the poor; even talking with church personnel could place people in danger. Everywhere, anxiety, fear, and distrust were palpable.

Carla wrote to her old advisor, Fr. Ganss:

> Our hope was to work with the Archdiocese of San Salvador, but with the situation being what it is, we have chosen to wait and accompany the people in the violent and confusing times. I feel at peace with the decision and trust that the Lord of Pilgrims will show us where we should be and how best we can serve the Church, the people and the Gospel.

> The readings of Easter Week where Jesus always says, "Be not afraid," I feel a bit of fear, not knowing what the future holds, but I believe it is a healthy fear and that the grace of the moment will not be lacking.

> I feel for my mother…and have acquired a deeper desire for life and living because of her example. However, I'm aware of my own poverty in being quite helpless to do anything for her.

To Grandma Ford, she wrote reassuringly: "Greetings from your adopted bird! I hope you have been comforted by the fact that El Salvador has been quite quiet lately. Yesterday I took a day of retreat in order to listen a bit to the Divine Circus Master and see what is the next act He wants. Today Ita is off reflecting. Luckily there still are Sisters who have big schools where we can go and be still in the private castle that houses the nuns.

"When you come before the Lord, ask with us to lead us to where we can best serve Him, His poor and this beat-up Church of El Salvador. I'm sure He hears our prayer—however, the waiting is getting to me a bit."

Carla wrote to several sisters to thank them for their solidarity after "little Oscar's" death, noting how much it had changed the road she and Ita would walk. Still, she placed her trust in the Divine Circus Master to lead the way.

In May she wrote to Regina McEvoy (of the Maryknoll leadership team) about the new challenges they faced, including the fact that they had no one place to stay: "The more I wander the more I admire Abraham! No wonder he had great faith—there's nothing stable to hold onto when one is forever moving. Maybe that's what it's all about. At least in Salvador it's a good way to identify with the valiant pueblo who has a spunky dynamic faith that will get it thru this Paschal mystery.

"I hope I can be faithful to all I receive. This change from Chile to here has been like a new life gift and a real shot in the arm to me. I suggest change for anyone slipping into complacency! Also I trust that more girls will be attracted to Saviorland."

Ita wrote to Rachel Lauze, MM: "The first month has really flown, as we're trying to get a feel for the country and church as well as looking for a place to hang our hats. Historically this is not the ideal time to arrive on the scene—but the Lord got us here for some reason. ...My friend and fellow pilgrim from Chile, Carla Piette, does her mental health by copying some of the stylized folk art that comes from a town called La Palma. This card is one of last night's clear-the-brain time."[16]

In mid-May Carla wrote to several Maryknoll sisters in Chile describing their challenge in El Salvador:

> Greetings to you shivering silhouettes from your sweating swingers! Needless to say, we have not been idle and I thank God that Maddie has a garden in which I can work up blisters to see me through this long wait. However, given the fact that the Lord is never mezquino [stingy], a lot of learning has gone on, about this insane situation in which we are present as well as about the faith of these spunky dynamic people who are aware of what is happening and I guess as ready as anyone can be for a war. Since the new law of arms has gone into effect, most people who are wounded and taken to the hospitals either disappear or are shot in the hospital so the latest craze is first aid courses on all sides.

The repression that this junta is applying is incredible. Since the first of this year more than 1,200 people of the pueblo have been killed. That doesn't include the security force numbers. The newspapers here look like anatomy books with pictures of the mutilated bodies found hither and yon. However, life continues to dolly on and the beautiful greeting of the Salvadoran people, "Primero Dios," kind of expresses where their hope lies. I've discovered a lot about my own faith in seeing and listening to them express their faith. I believe that the yes that I continue to say will contain the strength necessary for the surprises each day holds.

In one of our trips to the campo, Ita and I, along with a Salvadoran priest, two seminarians and a lady, were introduced to the way the soldiers search here. They are not quite as gentle or dumb as the Chilean boys. This was the first time I experienced the terrific hatred of the church and as we reflected later, they could have popped us off right there where so many campesinos have been killed that many pueblos [villages] in the area are completely abandoned. However, my own preoccupation was that the elastic on my pants was broken and with hands on wall and legs apart and ransacking of body it could have been deleterious to say the least. Thanks be to God and a safety pin that held, nothing funny happened.

Well, ladies, know you aren't forgotten, give my love to the girls. Sometimes I get very homesick for Chile, for friends, for roses, for what made Chile home for me for 15 years. It's good to feel—even homesick— and the rest is in the Circus Master's hands.

To Becky Quinn in Coelemu she wrote:

Today it is so hot. They say before the rain it gets very hot, and boy, it really is a winner today. I always heard that heat makes one passionate—gads—either

I have no passion in me or that's a stupid thought. Whenever I get to a point of complaining of heat I think of Chile—cold, damp, wet and layers of clothes—and I conform. But today is definitely hot.

The rumor is that the big war will come in about two months. Something has to come soon or this country will be destroyed by just the insane repression done by the army. Poor ole Ita has seen some horrible sights that, thank God, I have only shared thru her. However weak, limited and aware that this is quite raw and real, I'm for sticking it out. I believe that good will win over evil, that creativity will win over destruction and that Peace will win over war. How this will happen may be thru the whole death and resurrection suffered by the great majority, but my belief in Jesus who makes all things new is growing. God has never abandoned me—I've felt alone and lonely but I'm learning to wait and He is present even in this mess. I appreciate your prayers and letters very much. Give my love to all.

The country was growing ever more violent. On May 14, government forces slaughtered more than six hundred campesinos trapped at the Sumpul River, which separates El Salvador and Honduras. Women and girls were assaulted, and survivors testified that some infants had been thrown into the air and then shot, as if in target practice. Survivors also reported that gunfire came from helicopters and that Honduran soldiers at the river's edge blocked entry to Honduras, indicating coordination between the armies of both countries. That month, in addition to the May 14 massacre, army, security, and paramilitary forces killed 1,197 unarmed civilians, most of them from rural areas.[17]

On May 23 Carla wrote to friends in Chile that their assignment had finally been determined:

Greetings from the land of eternal sunrises now turned quite sad at the daily events of which you all are no doubt aware. Our investigations into possible jobs have come to a close since the situation is not one in which to begin Pastoral work. So we have been asked by the Vicar and the Religious to work fulltime in an Emergency committee doing the normal things in this abnormal situation...refugees, food, first aid, medicines, etc. I think we'll be working in the department of Chalatenango which is the most affected so far. We'll be living in the city of Chalatenango— the Vicar promises us a room in the rectory which also serves as a minor seminary. We're doing pretty good—trying to keep our mental health in spite of the sadness and the shoestring living.

In deciding what work to undertake, Carla and Ita noted that Archbishop Romero himself had stressed that priority should be given to assigning relief workers to assist refugees, especially in the mountainous Chalatenango area, where food, medicine, and evacuation transportation were critically needed. Fr. Cesar Jerez, Jesuit provincial superior for Central America who had initially encouraged Carla to serve in El Salvador, supported their decision.

The area of Chalatenango, one of the poorest and most dangerous in the northern zone close to the Honduran border, had been taken over as a training camp by the popular guerilla organizations and was therefore a major target for government forces. People trapped between the two armed groups could choose to join one side or the other—or flee to the hills while their houses, crops, and animals were destroyed by the Salvadoran army and the paramilitary ORDEN, created in 1964 to destroy political opposition in rural Salvador. Women and children hiding in the hills were in desperate need of food, supplies, and a safe place to go.

Even before the death of Archbishop Romero the people of Chalatenango had been harassed for their faith and loyalty to him. On at least one occasion while he was traveling to the towns and villages of the area to celebrate Mass, the army stopped and frisked him. Government forces set up roadblocks to keep people away, but they took back trails and filled the church.

Carla and Ita's work took them down a dangerous, unpredictable, lonely, and exhausting road. Communication was difficult. Since telephone lines and mail could not be trusted because of government surveillance, important messages had to be conveyed in person, which meant driving through hazardous military checkpoints. Despite their challenging schedule, Ita and Carla maintained their practice of regular fasting, prayers, and retreats at the Asunción Sisters school and convent in San Salvador.

The horrors they saw daily were overwhelming. On one day of Ita's rest at Santa Ana, huge army tanks suddenly roared through the town. Maddie called Ita to join her at the window but Ita declined, saying, "I can't—I'm in Bermuda today."

At the end of May, Ita wrote to her sister, Rene: "I'm taking a day off today to be alone. I think I'm supersaturated with horror stories and daily body count. I'm not sure how you get acclimated to a country that has an undeclared civil war going. Carla and I now have a job. We're the full-time workers of the emergency committee in the vicariate of Chalatenango. What this means is that the church of San Salvador is facing reality and getting ready to help with food, medicines and refugee centers. Carla keeps asking—how many dead make a war? What's the magic number?"[18]

Describing their work, Ita said, "It's a schizophrenic thing that such supplies [first aid kits and medicine] are considered 'war materials' by those who seem reluctant to admit that this is, in fact, a war."[19] Carla was diligent in hiding the first aid supplies to avoid detection by government forces.

On June 1 Ita sent to Peg Hanlon, Regina McEvoy, and the sisters in Chile and the Central American regions "Some Reflections Six Weeks After Arrival in El Salvador": "I don't know if it is in spite of or because of the horror, terror, evil, confusion, lawlessness, but I do know that it is right to be here, to activate our gifts, to use them in the situation, to believe that we are gifted in and for Salvador now, and that the answers to the questions will come when they are needed. To walk in faith one day at a time with the Salvadorans along a road filled with obstacles, detours and sometimes washouts—this seems to me what it means to be for us in El Salvador. It's a privilege to come to a Church of martyrs and people with a strong committed faith."[20]

In early June a friend from Chile, Jane Kenrick, stopped in El Salvador to visit Carla and Ita. She had great difficulty finding them, because they were on the move and stayed in so many places. With help, Jane found the Cleveland missioners; Dorothy and Jean then brought Carla and Ita to her. When they saw Jane, the two women burst into tears of joy. They told her that finding their role in El Salvador had been a terrible struggle, especially since it was dangerous for anyone to be seen as close to the Church. They said that their decision for refugee work in Chalatenango was definite. Dorothy told Jane, "Carla and Ita will be doing very dangerous work—I'm very afraid for them." The next day Carla and Ita accompanied Jane to San Salvador and warned her, "If people come on buses with guns, don't resist—these are bandits—they want what they can get." When they said good-bye, Ita and Carla told Jane that they didn't expect to see her again. "If anything happens to one of us, we pray that we both go—don't know how we'd do without the other," they said. Jane was distraught to realize that the women did not expect to survive. Jane, like Carla and Ita, had lived under Chile's military regime. She experienced El Salvador as far worse. Its atmosphere was one of total lawlessness and pervasive fear. In Chile, there was some pretense of justice; in El Salvador there was none.[21]

Carla wrote Becky that she and Ita had been robbed, but not harmed, by men with a machete and knife: "This is the third time since I've come that I've been robbed. It kind of loses its drama after awhile."

She also described a visit to Arcatao, a village that had been taken over by ORDEN. Only the supporters of the military and paramilitary groups lived there now. The parish team was not allowed to take food to refugees living in the country:

> The Srs had to leave because of the constant perse-
> cution of the Guardia—and the threats on their life.
> Gads, was that weird! The people in the town were
> mostly ORDEN—the group of extreme right—but
> they are the same humble, poor campesinos as those
> that they kill and call extremistos and Communists.
> During Mass as one looked around, one could see peo-
> ple with pistols on their belts and pencils, noting who
> was talking with Padre. The people wouldn't even
> give a glass of water to us—and we had to buy some
> tortillas for dinner. The Srs house had been robbed
> of big things—stove, refrigerator, beds, etc., and it's
> right across the street from the Guardia.

> Then on this Friday I went up with another group
> of Srs who have received a threat that if they don't
> leave their convent in 8 days, they'll be killed. So that
> was kind of sad for them to have to leave, but at least
> the people were a bit more human. The Vicar said a
> beautiful, strong Mass and explained the evil of the
> killings, the robbings, the calumny, etc. This place,
> Citala, is right on the Honduras border so naturally
> it's handy for either side.

> And life continues—Ita and I are working full time on
> the Emergency Committee of the department of Cha-
> latenango. At present we live between Santa Ana and
> the Asunción Srs in Chalatenango. However the Vicar
> will give us two rooms in the rectory so we will have
> a little independence. I'll be glad for that since always
> being a guest kind of gets to you after awhile.

Jose, an ex-seminarian who worked with the Maryknoll sisters during this time, later said of them, "They were happy,
rejoiced in the beauty of nature, lived in personal poverty,
sacrificing for others, ...continually searching in faith and
hope, preoccupied with the Beatitudes." He recalled that

Carla "fumed at the situation of celebrating a Mass in such a town [Arcatao] when the people were suffering in the hills." She made numerous attempts to get past armed checkpoints to deliver food and was stopped many times before she finally made it through. In the hills she saw children living in holes in the ground, heard them tell how soldiers invaded their village and killed their parents, their brothers and sisters. Jose recalled that Carla then said what he regarded as prophetic words: "That my blood may pay the price of this sin my society has committed."[22]

Carla wrote to Regina McEvoy in early June: "As yet we don't have a place of any stability which we can call our pad and prayer room, but as beat-up pilgrims, we are walking the road and trusting that needs will be met since we haven't been abandoned by the Lord of the Pilgrim. Isaias 43 is still my guideline... 'I am doing a new thing.'"

She also wrote to Padre Pedro Perez, her spiritual advisor in Chile:

> The Church of the base is strong, persecuted and massacred. Arcatao, where I visited, had 42 men catechists two years ago. They have all been tortured and killed without any burial.

> The hierarchical church is divided in such a way that no other Bishop except Bishop Rivera y Damas, who is the Administrator now, went to Archbishop Romero's funeral. If anyone wishes to have proof of the faith, it is to see the Church here and how the Salvadorans are sincere and frank while the Bishops say things that can only be lamented.

> The Church of the priests and religious is also awaiting a New Pentecost. Twelve priests have left their parishes in the last 3 months and have gone abroad for reasons of personal security (they have killed 8 priests) or to work with groups. Because of the scarcity of priests, in the parishes where there are religious, they do almost everything. This is a Church of courage with fear, with passion and hope of resurrection.

And what is my role in this bag of cats? I distribute food, clothing and medicine to the war victims here. There are 2,000 displaced families in Chalatenango where I work. Therefore, I look for the people in the hills and leave them food and am in the towns with the traitors of the groups. All are dying of hunger.

If you were here nearby, you would tell me to take a rest, as I am tired, and in two weeks time I hope to get to Nicaragua for a few days. Meanwhile, I send you greetings and prayers. Remember us in your prayers. With affection, Carla

Initially church teams had worked to recover, identify, and bury the many bodies dumped along country roads and city streets. Then in June notes that were pinned to the bodies warned, "If you bury this body, the same will happen to you." Jean Donovan wrote, "So many killings. I don't know if I can face another body. It may be that each day you get worn down a little."[23]

In mid-June, at the request of the San Salvador Archdiocese and the Ecumenical Committee for Humanitarian Aid, Carla and Ita sent an urgent petition to representatives of the U.S. Catholic Church, including Maryknoll, the U.S. Conference of Catholic Bishops, and several organizations dedicated to peace and justice: "Given the political situation of El Salvador, which is nothing less than an undeclared civil war, we urgently ask that your office petition the International Red Cross, Geneva, to recognize the existing state of war in El Salvador, so that International norms of behavior in times of war be respected and supervised: concretely—that hospital and refugee centers be respected as neutral centers and that humanitarian aid of food and medicines be allowed to enter the country. Without a declaration of war, the victims of repression or of the war itself cannot receive help from international humanitarian agencies."[24]

Carla and Ita circulated the petition to many contacts around the world. When Carla sent a copy to a sister in Peru, she wrote:

Being of the Emergency Committee has given us a good chance to know a lot of people as well as trust in the Lord of the Way since we don't have an example of what to do or how to do but rather just *do it* as best we can. Right now we're in the writing up projects stage, trying to get first aid courses going, giving parishes ideas on how best to organize, etc. It's not what I had in mind when I came but it definitely is needed and besides learning a lot, I'm getting a kick out of this gypsy living for the bigger Pastoral.

If you have contact with any organization there in Lima, I ask a favor of you: to ask them as a group to pressure the Red Cross in Geneva to recognize that Salvador is at war. Without this [declaration] horrible atrocities are being done like going into hospitals and taking people out, etc. and no international norms are respected or established. We have written to the USA asking this but you might know of more groups and better ones down there. Any news along this line is very welcome. Pray for us, please, that we may be "disponible" [ready] to serve this pueblo without fear of consequences.

Carla wrote me a lengthy letter with the same urgent plea. (Even in the midst of the horrors, she remembered my upcoming birthday.) Her letter vividly described current atrocities and detailed the need for Red Cross involvement; she hoped that my contacts with a local peace and justice group might help. The urgency of her appeal and her graphic descriptions terrified and appalled me:

Without this announcement, no hospitals, schools, refugee centers or churches are respected and now they are definitely not respected. It's unbelievable how people are shot right in the hospitals, churches are machine-gunned, kids are killed in the classrooms, and all because they may be a member of a family that may belong to one of the popular leftist groups.

I pray that I not get hardened to the atrocities I experience, and I pray each day for the conversion of the USA, like we used to pray for the conversion of Russia. If the USA intervenes in a military way here, this whole Central American block will turn into another Vietnam—gads. Already dear ole Uncle Sam has furnished the barbaric Salvadoran army with equipment used to kill innocent farmers, children and youth. It's unbelievable but over 2,000 people have been killed since Jan 1, 1980, by the repressive govt here called "Christian Democrat."

I never really had much hope in little groups in the States pushing for justice since I saw the US govt as a monstrous war machine that stepped on little countries with no criteria or control. However here the people DO believe in the power of the pueblo—the people of the US—to stop a possible US intervention, so I believe with the pueblo. I trust that you will do what you can—I ask no more.

My work here is with the Emergency Committee preparing for war and the aftermath. It's a constant pilgrimage of being led here and there to see needs and bring the info to the archdiocesan office and write letters and generally proceed from one moment to the next. That's why that [International] Red Cross deal is so important. Two weeks ago 25 people were killed and the police wouldn't let anyone bury them. The Red Cross wouldn't go because they said they only did that in times of war. So the families of the 25 watch them being eaten by vultures and a typhoid epidemic is in full swing. This isn't a very jolly letter but it's a real one. Please write again soon if just a postcard to say you got this.

From this point on, I was frantic, desperately worried, and anxiously praying for my friend's safety. I wrote to our local congressman, Clement Zablocki, then chairman of the

House Foreign Affairs Committee, and enclosed a copy of Carla's appeal. Zablocki did take steps to investigate, but complete responses to his requests arrived only after Carla's death.[25]

Carla described their situation to Becky in mid-June: "I finally have a Christian community here. The people here are aware and alert—everyone is very suspicious, words must be measured here, and real wisdom is the need of the moment. In a country where people are killed for going to a meeting or associating with key people. This is a heavy load...genocide and crazy which makes life very intense. I just pray that my words are truth and if death comes to me or to others it was in alliance with truth."

In July Carla's letter to Grandma Ford assured her that she and Ita were well and still "able to laugh." She invited Mrs. Ford to spend her November birthday with them or perhaps come for a few days after the November assembly of sisters in Nicaragua. Then, she wrote, "we'll be all rested and beautiful!"

In mid-July she wrote to another sister: "Ole beat-up Salvador is not absorbing all of my energies, but it's doing a good job of trying to! I've never been in a situation so hostile to the Church and so full of mistrust. The Word of God that I always read and chewed on has suddenly become a very real promise as I dolly along with the Words as the only security in this insane atmosphere. However, being the perverse clown that I am, I'm here at this time and I hope to get a few more clowns since we're at present four in this whole little bouillon cube country."

Carla described her work to her mother's cousin, Sr. Catherine Verbeten:

> Since I've been here the repression and genocide has increased to unbelievable proportions. Many times I've said I'd be afraid to leave here, lest I'd have to adapt all over again to living in this situation of war, persecution and vengeance.
>
> This may sound strange to you, but as the repression and genocide continues here, it becomes harder

and harder to do pastoral work. So what do I do? I drive people places—like other Srs who are more and more afraid to stay in the isolated parts of the country areas. I drive Caritas food to refugees of which there are 2,000 families in the Dept of Chalatenango. I go to meetings where needs are expressed and frustrations aired and in the end very little accomplished.

I've come to appreciate what Jesus means when He says "I am the way." The way here is daily changing as one tries to respond to this genocidal situation. In one parish where there are no longer priests or Srs because of the situation, there were 42 adult catequists— all 42 have been brutally murdered. No one wants to be a catequist anymore since it usually means your life and yet we try to attend these remote parts of the country. That's where I drive priests who can't drive. This weekend I go up to Arcatao where the 42 were killed. We hope to bring food for 50 families.

Thank you for the news on Mama. I still try to preferentially visit the old and talk with them, since people like yourself do that with Mama. In my old age I see how different are the Lord's ways from ours and in my effort to accept His present passion, I feel I'm being healed.

In El Salvador Carla continued her habit of giving nicknames to her colleagues. Maddie became Mother Goose; Ita remained Ernestina. She did not hesitate to give nicknames to the "hot priests" (those under threat from government forces) whom she drove to godforsaken places. Padre Fabian Amaya, vicar of the department of Chalatenango, became Padre Oso—Father Teddy Bear—because of his hefty build. Padre Sigfredo Salazar, a polite man who frequently bowed with a sincere "at your service," became known to everyone as Su Servidor. He later said, "God gave us the power to name creatures, and Carla exercised that power."

The work of transporting food, supplies, and refugees was physically demanding. Carla often lugged hundred-pound sacks of food; she joked with Ita that she really should belong to the stevedores union. Simply driving La Tonquita on the badly rutted roads and paths took a lot of strength, and every trip also meant facing the dangers of the military searches. Each day brought new urgent challenges.

On July 20, 1980, Carla and Ita sent an extensive, blunt report to the Maryknoll leadership team and to Maryknoll Central America and Chile regions. The report made clear what a difficult road they were walking, day by day, hour by hour, as they tried to meet the people's emergency needs without a clear road map, without rural experience, and without an extensive community of support. Their description of the challenges they were facing brought welcome messages of encouragement and support from many sisters throughout Maryknoll, particularly their friends in Chile.

They described the political situation, the escalation of repression and violence since their arrival, and the challenge of determining how they could best serve.

> For the last three months we have had no house of which we could say, "This is our home." Because we arrived at a time when the Church was in mourning and struggling to respond to the problems of daily persecution, we find it difficult to find someone with whom to reflect on this experience. We are pastoral workers used to having people whom we can visit, meet with, etc. Now we have no people—we cannot visit because of the times and the very real fear of placing others in danger because of belonging to the church, which is one of the security force's biggest enemies. A certain spontaneous support from the Sisters has been present in notes and prayers. However, given the war situation, our reduced numbers and recent illness of one member here, we have felt quite isolated and alone. Control of the mails as well as of the phones makes it difficult to communicate what is happening here, and your letters are not arriving too frequently. We feel the need of more palpable solidarity.

Besides lacking our own home, a stable salary, local church and tangible regional support and inventing a job daily, neither one of us are emotional or psychological giants in this crazy situation. We realize that a lot of our energies just go into trying to keep walking down this dark road without becoming as dark as the situation.

WHAT DO WE REALLY DO?
1. We continue to seek out dialogue and collaboration with humanitarian groups, do translations and give in petitions for aid.
2. We drive priests to outlying country districts.
3. We drive food to contacts who will get it to people hiding from the security forces or the popular groups.
4. We transport refugees and clothes to different hiding places.
5. We try to visit Maddie in Santa Ana once a week.
6. We meet as an area twice a month.
7. We accompany Religious who are alone at present.
8. We do an infinite amount of [government bureaucracy] paper work to stay in this nutsy country.

Carla and Ita recommended that additional sisters could be sent to work with Maddie in Santa Ana, an urban area where "Maddie's ministry has credibility with the people." They did not believe that another sister should join them in their emergency refugee work "until the situation in Chalatenango has more shape to it."

The last reflection we want to share is what we have learned in this experience:
1. A total dependence and trust in God.
2. A deepening of our commitment and availability.
3. A coming to know the pastoral agents of the local church and other missioners.
4. An opportunity to know this situation of repression and all its consequences.

5. An exercise in humility and faith.
6. A coming to know one's personal limitations and basic psychological needs.
7. An awareness of ability to adapt to incredible situations.

On July 24 Carla wrote to Becky Quinn and Ceci Santos:

> This time has been wild as well as trying. Our main work has been chofering priests to Godforsaken places, driving food to Godforsaken people and trying not to feel Godforsaken ourselves. I'm planning a little trip to Nicaragua in two weeks, just to sleep, since we sleep in an average of five different beds a week. Such is the life of the pilgrim and the poor.
>
> Peg Healy came to visit us after her visit to Nicaragua's celebration. We send with her a report that she'll send to Chile. It's full of our blood, sweat and tears of the past three months.
>
> The Lord definitely leads us over the roughest roads and steepest paths. Yet deep down I believe this is where I should be. Thank God I'm strong of health and body—poor ole Ita is having her bouts with bugs and the different food reactions and the hard life. When I think of it really, next to the 1000s of refugees living in the mountains, what we live is nothing. I count on your prayers and your letters—someday we'll be able to laugh again and say, "what a crazy circus we're in."

By late July the needs of the Chalatenango refugees, particularly the children, had grown so great that Jean Donovan began to travel with Carla to deliver Caritas food and to move women and children to safe havens.

Chris Rody of the Cleveland mission team greatly admired Carla's patience with the refugee women and her respect for them. She described an occasion when a group of peasant women were agonizing about whether they should move from one refugee center to another across town where they were told their children were staying. The women had already fled from violence in their villages and were still frightened and paralyzed by distrust. Chris recalled, "Carla had a tremendous sense of respect for the needs of the women, treating them not as commodities to be moved around but as people with sensitivities. We waited [for nearly two hours] until the women decided among themselves and then we took them, without incident."[26]

On July 30 Carla wrote to Grandma Ford:

Little bits of news have been trickling down here that you are very concerned about Ita. Now I would say that you are falling down on your part of the bargain—to trust the Lord totally—and I will write you to assure you that all is well.

Well, your idle bird had a jolly encounter with the mules as we joined an expedition to bring food up a rather difficult road. Dear ole Ernestina Ford held the reins so well that the stubborn mules went each their own way (we each walked 2 mules) Ernestina is being pulled rather dialectically. Finally I screamed, "Ita, let go for Pete's sake!" and the strain was reduced. In that escapade it was quite obvious that little light foot Ford was in condition for mountains more than Tootsie Roll Piette was.

The work seems to be taking more shape as time goes on. This is a blessing since our frustration level was just about reached. As you know, I take it out on everything, but ole neat and tidy Ford takes it out on Carla, so we went thru some stormy days. However, I know the Lord is with us in this storm, and good people like yourself pray for us so we sing, "If God is for us, who can be against..." Don't forget my invite to come down, grandma, I'll bet you'd love it!

She also wrote to Kathy Gilfeather, MM, in Chile:

> Your words were so consoling and I must admit it's
> been rather different here from Chile. Civil war is
> messy—no doubt about that. It's also frustrating when
> one is of the church—God who is for people and not
> for this side or that. At present I am chofering for a
> young priest who has been threatened. I drive alimen-
> tos [food] to different refugee places, talk with differ-
> ent people, carry on and on and on with the Lord on
> what is happening with this valiant pueblo.
>
> We were involved in getting two guerillas out of hos-
> pital—11 and 12 years old—since in the morning an
> 8 year-old guerilla was machine-gunned in hospital.
> Those are the things that just confuse and frustrate.
> However, the Salvadorans are sharp and strong and
> have nerves of steel. In one place in the campo in the
> middle of Mass when the shooting started, the wom-
> en just got up, looked around and kneeled down. The
> men closed the doors and the priest who I drive, Sig-
> fredo [Su Servidor] just stood and waited and then
> continued Mass. No hysteria, no leaving church, just
> a bit of commotion as Carla sits on bench and looks
> around and says inside, "What have I come to?" It's a
> barrel of laughs, especially as this priest who I chofer
> says, "Step on the gas" over roads that even Toyota
> Jeep ads wouldn't come near to describe.
>
> So—the walk continues and the Lord of the Way leads
> each day with no map and no clear weather but rather
> fog and total trust. But after it all—like Peter, I'm glad
> I jumped out of the boat and said, "If it's you, Lord,
> bid me to come." And He says, "Come." So I dolly
> on the waves, sinking, screaming out, but holding His
> hand and I know He's here and I'm glad I am.

In August Ita and Carla finally had a place of their own:
a small area of plywood cubicles inside the parish store-
room in Chalantenango. They named it El Camino Real

after a fancy hotel in San Salvador. Ita described their place in a letter to Connie Pospisil: "Actually, we live in a sala of the parish—but now it has a door and some plywood divisions for bedrooms. Showers and johns are in the patio—and there's a kitchen 'next door.' There are about a dozen or so residents in the parish and the number fluctuates on weekends and people use it as a halfway house as they look for refuge. It's quite an experience of extended if not integrated community."

Refugees stayed at the parish house temporarily while waiting for safe transport to established refugee centers. Army quarters and a police station were almost adjacent to the parish house, facing the same plaza as the cathedral.

While Joan Petrik was on a visit home, Terry Alexander learned that the police had been asking suspicious questions about her, and the sisters decided that it would not be safe for Joan to return. On August 5 Maura Clarke, MM, who had previously served in Nicaragua, arrived to join the mission team.

In August Peter Hinde, a Carmelite priest, and Betty Campbell, a nurse and Sister of Mercy with earlier mission experience in Peru, also joined Carla, Ita, and others on the Archdiocesan Pro-Refugee Team. In addition to their refugee service, Hinde and Campbell worked with the Salvador Commission for Human Rights to document the violence through the accounts of refugee-survivors of massacres.[27]

Ellen McDonald, MM, visited the sisters on behalf of Maryknoll's Central Governing Board, whose members were already concerned for their safety, particularly after receiving Carla and Ita's three-month report. Ellen encouraged each sister—Maddie, Terry, Carla, Ita, and Maura—to feel free to leave, given the climate of violence and threats. Each woman chose to remain.

Carla's last letter to Grandma Ford, again bolstering her spirits, was written on August 11:

> Now for the report on our actions. We've been transporting refugees and "hot" priests to different coun-

try areas. I believe that the Lord protects us and no harm will come to us. This is a unique experience and I admit I do try to protect Ita although she doesn't like that. As far as risk goes—I never invite her to accompany me in a risky thing I may be doing, although she protests strongly. In this insane situation, who's to know what is risky, and actually all we're doing is very humanitarian.

If you have a Bible, read Chapter 43 of Isaias ["Do not be afraid..."]—that's my strength and confidence. Our little house within a house is taking shape and I'd say it's a real experience of integrated community. Ita is good at keeping all our accounts straight. I feel like the broad back of the team—dragging food hither and yon and being totally disorganized which of course drives Ernestina nuts.

We felt quite alone as far as Maryknoll's contact but recently had some visitors which did a lot to boost up the lagging spirits. There is no way to rationalize our being here except that God wants us here—and of that both of us are sure. Sometimes I feel almost unworthy to work with such valiant poor people. At other times I feel so happy to learn so much here and participate in this struggle. Then again I am aware of my own poverty and how the Lord fills up what is lacking in me, in my strength and in my disposition.

There is a certain freedom for me since contact with my family is so minimal. I always say to Ita that if anything happens to me—she has only to advise Maryknoll, but should she be harmed, I dread having to advise the Ford Foundation, although I appreciate you all very much.

The time of the crunch could be getting closer and communication may be difficult or impossible. Please know that we trust in the Lord of Life and I expect you to do the same. I know that you are a woman of faith and that gives me strength—so like Sara, Abraham's wife—let's believe that out of the sterility of hard times, a whole new being will be born and we will have participated.

I said to Ita....if I had to choose another name, I'd choose Rahab [Joshua Ch 2] who also did her best to defend life. Give my love to Billy, Maryanne [Billy's wife], and Rene and a special hug to you, Grandma.

Jean Donovan kept a daily journal that documented much of the violence and killings. In August, when she often worked with Carla to distribute supplies and transport refugees, her journal described an escalation of violence in Chalatenango. On August 9: "Carla relocated four families, one child was shot in the hospital, and five bodies were found on the road to the airport." On August 13: "Violence bad in Chalatenango. 40 soldiers killed in a truck in San Antonio." On August 14: "Helicopters, trucks and soldiers very active in Chalatenango." Jean wrote that Chalatenango was absolute civil war—bodies lying all over. On August 21 she helped Carla move more refugees.[28]

Carla wrote to Becky: "We're moving refugees, zipping food around, comforting survivors of bombing and taking hot priests to hot places, I love the circus and can imagine that Chile would be very boring after this. However, I try to live one day at a time and be open to what the Lord has in store.... I leave the future in the Circus Master's hands."

She wrote Fr. Ganss, regretting that her check for Jesuit Studies had not gotten through and hoping that she could read back copies next year when she would visit home and make another Ignatian retreat in Oshkosh. Then she added:

Your words are very strengthening, Fr. Ganss. This country is absolutely wild and the other Sister and myself are in a very hot spot—Chalatenango. Our work is getting food to people—refugees, getting the refugees moved from unsafe places, driving priests who are threatened to out of the way places, and in general doing crazy things to help these repressed people live in an insane violent situation.

I have come to believe very much in the Lord's word that He leads us and gives us strength and courage for incredible tasks. I believe His Spirit is with us and that no harm will come to us until He permits this to happen. The great privilege of serving the suffering church is one of the greatest graces of my vocation. We work with the Salvadoran priests and religious of the Dept. of Chalatenango and all of them are beautiful, dedicated people who are in a state of mourning seeing their people so repressed and killed. I am grateful for your prayer and words. The prophet Isaias is my strength, especially Chapters 40 onward. My mother continues in the nursing home and I trust that the Lord who never abandons His poor and little ones will not abandon her.

Her letter reached Fr. Ganss on the day she died.

***

For many years Carla had prayed for a "heart of stone." On August 21, after they had prayed "I will take away your hearts of stone and give you hearts of flesh" (Ezekiel 36:26), Carla said to Ita, "I've come miles since then and you've walked a lot of that road with me." "Now," she added, "you can dismiss your servant in peace, O Lord."

Later that day Carla drove to San Salvador and prayed with the Asunción Sisters and at Romero's tomb in the cathedral. The next day she spent time in private fasting and retreat, as she and Ita regularly did, at the Ascunción Sisters' convent. She also spoke to the senior high-school girls from wealthy families at the Colegio de la Asunción about missionary service, warning them not to do charity work without also working for justice. They were puzzled by her quote from St. Vincent de Paul: "We should apologize to the poor for our charity toward them." She stopped at the seminary to load up on medicines for the parish in Chalatenango.

Peter Hinde remembered his visit with Carla that day:

Carla was in good spirits. She said that as a North American she had been feeling the weight of the social sin against the people, the involvement of her own U.S. government in supporting and aiding the repression. She could now see that the refugee assistance, coupled with her solidarity with the people, was a way both of countering the sinful structures that tarnish all U.S. citizens and a way of disassociating herself from U.S. government policy.

She had spent the retreat in fasting, as well as prayer, because, as she said, "Such devils as are wandering around this country can only be cast out by prayer and fasting."

We asked her if she was writing back to the U.S. about what was happening in the Chalatenango area, as she had often done recently. "No, I see so much violence and death...the worst of brutality...that my mind becomes empty and I can't bring myself to write." As she drove off she said, "The people have to win...the people will win."[29]

The following day, Saturday, August 23, Carla drove Padre Su Servidor to several rural communities to say Mass and deliver food and medicine packets. Meanwhile, Ita met with a local army colonel (who, she said, "had labeled the Church 'subversive' because it's on the side of the weak") to petition, as she often did, for the release of missing persons. The colonel chose to release several prisoners that day, including a young man from San Antonio de Los Ranchos.

Among the refugees staying at the parish center were five families who had fled San Antonio de Los Ranchos after government forces—in reprisal for the community's protest against the Army's request to quarter a National Guard unit in their town—invaded the area, killed four people, and took the men prisoner. Some of the women refugees recognized the man the colonel released as a member of ORDEN who had betrayed their families. They told Ita, "Don't let him see us. He is a spy and will tell all where we are." Terrified that he would betray them, they begged her not to let him remain in the area.[30]

When Carla returned to Chalatenango early that evening, she agreed with Ita they should take the man to his village, a journey through guerilla-held territory. So, although night was coming and rain threatened, Carla and Ita set off in La Tonquita with the released man, accompanied by Esteban and Alfredo, two young seminarians, for a half-hour drive. Within ten minutes, it began to rain heavily.

Ita recalled, "We had the choice of two roads. One has no rivers along it but it had a lot of landslides [and we thought] the other was the better way to go, the one where you cross the same El Chapote River about five times." They had crossed four of the river bends when the water in the riverbed suddenly rose so high that Carla decided they could go no further. They let the prisoner out and told him that he would have to walk the rest of the way home. The seminarians jumped out to help turn the jeep around and were caught in the raging waters of a flash flood. Carla cried, "We are being taken." As the force of the water rolled the jeep onto the driver's side, Carla pushed Ita out the open window on the uppermost passenger's side just before the river swept the jeep away.

Ita barely survived. The rushing water carried her far downstream before she was able to grab a tree root and, after many attempts, claw her way up the slippery riverbank; there she collapsed, her body battered by the flood waters and bruised by the rocks. When the townspeople found her early the next morning, she was dehydrated as well. Later she reflected that now she, like the poor campesino refugees, had slept in the hills. The first aid kit used for her was one she and Carla had assembled just days before.

Alfredo and Esteban, strong young men, were bruised but otherwise unharmed. Despite the danger from government forces, they joined the townspeople in searching all night for Carla and Ita.

Late Sunday morning the local Red Cross found Carla's body—stripped naked by the force of the torrent and battered by the rocks—about twelve miles downstream. The rescuers carried her home. Bishop Rivera y Damas, with ten priests, said a Mass in Chalatenango for her that afternoon. The townspeople held a wake until midnight during which the peasants, already calling her "Martyr of Charity," gave testimony and sang songs. Even refugees whose names were on death lists came to pay their respects. Peter Hinde and Maura Clarke conducted a prayer reflection over Carla's body in the church that evening. Additional Masses were celebrated in the town that night and early Monday morning. The archdiocese managed to find a special casket for Carla, one long enough for her five feet eight inches—but even so, her shoes did not fit. She was buried in her rainbow dress.

Missioner Chris Rody described the wake:

> Last night as I stood honor guard by the bruised and broken body, undisguised by undertaker's cosmetics, I watched the simple people of Chalatenango and its neighboring pueblos pass by—it seemed like the wake ritual of Archbishop Romero—in what was done— church benches put sideways to keep the flow of people in order; the Mass and prayer services the entire night; and the flowers and candles.

> Some of the touching gestures: people touching the glass cover on the top half of the coffin and then kissing their fingers, the Sisters of Assumption making sure we have coffee and food—and most of all, the little old lady dressed all in black who—during the rosary—rested her arms and head on the corner of the coffin and took a little snooze.

Ita, although severely exhausted and in need of medical attention, insisted on helping to plan her friend's funeral liturgy. She knew it would be Carla's wish to be buried in the little village cemetery of the "beat-up little people."

She chose a reading from Romans, "Nothing can separate us from the love of God," and another from the Gospel of John, "Greater love hath no man than to lay down his life for his friends." On Monday afternoon the Chalatenango church was filled for the official burial Mass. "Loudspeakers echoed the words out over the army trucks and armored cars parked on the cement apron at the very front door of the Church to resound off the front of the army garrison facing on the same plaza," wrote Peter Hinde. Several Salvadorans who had worked with Carla gave testimony, describing her as *fogosa* (fiery). One young deacon spoke at length about the social teaching of the Church, the Scriptures, the words of Romero and of Carla. Jose, the ex-seminarian, recalled her fury on behalf of the people who suffered at the hands of the government's forces.[31]

The whole town accompanied the funeral procession to the cemetery. The road was downhill and somewhat slippery. Jean, who walked in front of the coffin, later said she felt as if Carla was still pushing her. Ita, behind the coffin, said she suddenly realized that it was the last time she would have to hold Carla back.

Because Carla's funeral was held quickly, some missioners and representatives from Maryknoll did not arrive in time. However, several Maryknoll sisters were able to come later to comfort and support Ita and Maura, and to learn more about the accident and the whole unpredictable, dangerous scene. Jessie Poynton came from Chile; Peg Hanlon visited on behalf of the sisters' leadership team. Carla's sister, Betty, devastated by her death, felt unable to make the trip.

On her return to New York, Peg Hanlon told the sisters at Maryknoll that she was stunned at the contrast between the beauty of the country and its people and the ugliness and suffering of the war. She was most amazed at Carla's lack of possessions: "It was a very, very radical poverty that she lived." Her clothes included a sweater from Chile, two little blouses, and her rainbow dress, which she wore much of the time. She had likely given everything else to the poor. Carla's colorful folk art paintings—many of Salvadoran birds, one weeping a river of tears—decorated the plywood walls of her room.

Everywhere she went Peg met people who wanted to tell her about Carla and what she had meant to them. "All the people we talked to—refugees and bishops, seminarians and cooks—all spoke to us of the special gift they had found in knowing Carla, for however short a time. She brought some meaning into their lives as she lived the mystery of being alive in that country at this time." Within days, the sisters heard of the first baby who was named after Carla.

Several more liturgies commemorated Carla's life: at Maryknoll on September 3, 1980, where her older brother, Jim, represented the Piette family; in the main cathedral of Santiago, with many of the people from La Bandera, where a banner proclaimed in Spanish one of Carla's favorite refrains: "We only did what we were supposed to do." (Luke 17:10); at St. Mary's Parish in Appleton, where my mother and I attended with Carla's family and friends. The hometown priest spoke highly of Carla's life, calling her a prophet in modern times. Carla's mother, now 81 and confused by dementia, did not attend the service. Her family visited her at her nursing home later that day to tell her of Carla's death, which she could not fully comprehend.

Each year on August 23 the people of San Antonio de Los Ranchos and of Chalatenango remember Carla with a ceremony at the river where she died. In 2000, twenty years after her death, Padre Alfredo Rivera, one of the seminarians in the jeep that night, spoke: "I feel the strength and the inspiration of Carla. I thank you for her. For me Carla is not dead. She is still with me, inspiring my work. I feel that Carla had the determination to save the lives of others. She and Ita and Maura comforted many of the people and gave them spirit and hope. They live in the people who remember them, who want the country to be different than it is. Knowing them helped me to go on to follow the vocation to the priesthood. And like them, I am committed to working with the poor."

Melinda Roper, president of the Maryknoll sisters in 1980, said at the 2000 memorial: "Carla had a deep sense of being a pilgrim on a journey. She was on call by day and night. She was, no doubt, a person who was evangelized by the poor themselves. She understood the Gospel from their standpoint, as well as from her own weaknesses. ... Perhaps, most important, is that she would be considered by the people to have been 'one of them,' to have been their 'friend.'"

The tributes might be summed up by Jessie Poynton's words: "She lived what she proclaimed."

***

Since receiving her desperate plea for Red Cross intervention in June, I had kept Carla in the back—and often the front—of my mind. On the night of August 23 I awoke suddenly from a vivid dream—a telegram from Carla that said, "I'm coming home." I shook my husband awake. "Tony, Tony, she's coming home! She's safe!!" I felt such relief, such joy! The next morning, a small story in the Milwaukee Sentinel reported, "Wisconsin Nun Drowns." It was indeed a coming home.

A month before her forty-first birthday, Carla died as, years earlier, she had prayed she might. "She always said she wanted to die at forty and to leave the world as she came into the world—born naked, no possessions," recalled a sister who knew her during her early years in Chile.

Fr. Ganss, at St. Louis University, received Carla's last letter on the day she died. In Wisconsin Sr. Michaeleen, our old grade-school friend, noticed that Carla's gift, the special Chilean candle that Michaeleen rarely lit, burned out completely on the night of August 23. She learned only later that Carla had died that night and said, "I grieved that death for such a long time."

In Indiana, Shirley Duane Alveal, a former Maryknoll colleague in Chile, had recently received a card from Carla in which she spoke of the extreme dangers and violence in El Salvador and said, "I feel the river calling me."[32]

Kathy Gilfeather, in Chile, recalled words in Carla's last letter: "I'm glad I jumped out of the boat and said, 'if it's you Lord, bid me to come' and He says, 'come.' So I dolly on the waves, sinking, screaming out but holding His hand and I know He's here and I'm glad I am."

Sheila Cassidy, in England, remembered Carla's 1976 meditation on Psalm 23, "Near restful waters He leads me." She also remembered the quip Carla had sent her in 1976: "It's a marvelous thing to be on a journey, not knowing where you are going, especially if you trust the cabbie!"

Ita had barely survived her own ordeal and was hospitalized for dehydration and exhaustion after Carla's funeral. As she recovered physically, she faced the emotional and spiritual pain of the loss of her dear friend, colleague, and partner in prayer.

In mid-October Ita wrote to Maryknoll to ask for financial help to replace the damaged La Tonquita, still parked in Chalatenango; she said the sight of it was "my reality therapy daily." Later, meeting the young prisoner they had been transporting the night Carla died, she pointed to the battered jeep and urged him to embrace a life of meaning and to appreciate Carla's life and sacrifice.

After Ita recovered, she wrote to me: "I know you were a friend that Carla kept in touch with. In fact, there was a letter from you dated August 6 among several on her desk. Carla and I were together since 1973—Chile—until she gave me a push through the jeep window and the current took me from her. In God's mysterious love, I survived the river and that night Carla experienced life in its fullness. Many of us are just left humble and creature-like in the face of that. I'm sending you the memorial card which is a custom here—as a small reminder of a most wonderful person, friend and missionary. Sincerely, Ita Ford"

Ita also thanked the many friends and colleagues who sent condolences. To all of us, she wrote, Carla's "death has meaning because her life was full of meaning. May the same be true for us."

She sent Betty her own condolences, along with several crosses and family pictures that Carla had kept, including one of Carla and Ita together, noting that Carla favored it because in it she "looked a little like Betty."

On September 7 Ita sent a long letter to the Maryknoll sisters of the Chile region. In it she stressed the importance of Carla's formative years in Chile and said: "Already she's a little bit larger than life, a heroine, 'an angel of charity.' I guess it's useless for me to protest that my beat up old friend is an example of God's strength being manifested in our weakness; His goodness and love through our vessels of clay."

Ita Ford's Letter to the
Maryknoll Sisters of the Chile Region
September 1980

WHEN SOMEONE DIES we all get together, cry, tell stories, laugh, reminisce, pray, have a liturgy and celebrate the fullness of life. And I know you all did that, so many of you who have known and loved Carla longer than I. What hit me was that there is no one in this country that knows Carla for longer than four months. She did already have some relationships because this is a country where there's very little superficiality. But it's just so different (for me) than if she had died in Chile. Already she's a little bit larger than life, a heroine, "an angel of charity." I guess it's useless for me to protest that my beat up old friend is an example of God's strength being manifested in our weakness; His goodness and love through our vessels of clay.

The Carla of El Salvador was a Chilean import. She claimed to be a product of Chile—15 years worth—and what she could offer came from her life experience there... you all know Carla's history, the ups and downs, the pain and the resurrections. What I want to share is something we talked about the Thursday before her death. The reading was, "I will take away your hearts of stone and give you hearts of flesh." (Jer. 31, 29-31) She said to me, "God has really done that for me."

A couple of years ago she told me that... in Chile... she asked for a heart of stone. She never really explained the whole thing, but I presumed it was a very painful situation and the only way to handle it was to shut off all feelings. Well, I guess you can just do that for so long and then you have to start working with them or God intervenes in some way. You all know the history, the years with Teresa Corquera, the family problems, all of it. But in that something was happening. The stone got porous, and then fleshy. She told me, "God has really done it. I now have a heart of flesh." And the heart ached for what's going on here. A lot of nights after coming home from listening to horror stories or consoling people she'd get her "toys," her magic markers, and some paper and begin to draw. She would draw birds crying and their tears forming mountain streams. She would draw wounded doves of peace. She would draw the Salvadoran countryside of cornfields going up the mountains. She also wrote a couple of songs, one, "You Are the Lord of the Road," was sort of our theme song as we set out with a Jeep loaded down with sacks of food and medicine.

As we continued talking, she said to me, "You walked a lot of that road with me." Then she said, "Now you can dismiss your servant in peace, Lord." (Lk.3) I thought she was referring to me, so I said, "I'm not so sure I get dismissed so easily." She answered, "We'll see."

That along with her letter to Kathy may or may not indicate that Carla had some kind of intuition that soon she would be with the Lord. (I'm sure I would have been the last person she would have told—given the circumstances) but we had talked about dying several times. (It seems to be a topic you can't avoid in El Salvador.) I think we both accepted the possibility as part of our being here. ...

After being here for a while, Carla couldn't help but be known in some circles. Her initiative, her firecrackers at meetings, her knocking heads with a machista Church, her putting her body where her mouth was, just being Carla, certainly did an awful lot to help earn us credibility in a difficult and disturbing ambiente. Yet, she wasn't superwoman nor was she doing crazy things. Anything that we did that was the least bit shaky or maybe shady, we checked it out first with the vicar.

Her Adamic streak of naming people and things was

very strong here. And most were quite apt. I can't say I gloried in her last name for me. It was "Mrs. Coathanger" because I lost some weight.

We caused quite a stir in New York with our three-month evaluation, that wasn't our intent. It was merely to ask for some input and help in a difficult situation. Some of you instinctively must have recognized that, because there were almost weekly letters to Carla from Rebecca, and Ceci almost as often. Others of you, too, have written. It's not the receiving or not of letters. It was just some sort of void where we couldn't feel your support, even though we felt part of the Chilean region and somehow sent by you. Marge Lyons sent a letter from NY that sort of captured it. We went through a very hard time and, I think, Carla was working herself up to return in January for the meeting—and probably with a firecracker or two. (I really don't know if you're safe or not!)

After not being alone for twelve days (I was even accompanied to the hospital), I'm just taking some time alone at the Asuncionistas to let the pain and hurt come out. It's one of those mysteries to be asked to mourn alone when everyone else with whom Carla shared life is in Chile, NY, even Bangladesh. But that seems to be the present script. Next week we'll be going to Guatemala to join the Sisters there in a retreat. I think that's a good idea. After that, Maura Clarke and I will go back to Chalatenango. Maura's great gift of kindness and love will be great for the traumatized, hurting people there. She'll be great for me, too.

I keep counting on your love and support, even though, I, too, am a poor correspondent.

Much love to each of you, Ita

Acknowledgements

I wish first of all to acknowledge my indebtedness to Robert Pelton, CSC, Professor of Theology; Director Emeritus, Institute for Pastoral and Social Ministry; Director, Latin American/North American Church Concerns; and fellow at the Kellogg Institute for International Studies at Notre Dame. The assistance of Father Pelton, known for his strong commitment to women in service in Latin America, was invaluable in facilitating publication of Carla's story. I thank him for his wise counsel and energetic support.

Writing Carla's story began as an act of personal remembrance. My telling of her story has been greatly enriched by the testimony of the Maryknoll sisters and former sisters who knew her, particularly those who worked with her in Chile. I thank Joan Ratermann, MM, for her constant encouragement and for introducing me to many sisters at Maryknoll who served in Chile. I am especially grateful to Maryknoll Sisters Jeanne Rancourt, Carol Marie McDonald, Kathleen Higgins, Marge Lyons, Cecilia Vandal, and Mary Ann Junas. Richard Brooker, MM, generously shared his memories and photographs.

E-mail correspondents Jessie Poynton, MM, and Connie Pospisil, MM, Jane Kenrick, RSM, Liz Gilmore, SHCJ, and Shirley Duane Alveal provided me with descriptions of life in Santiago poblaciones during the Pinochet years. Mauro and Carrol Pando, former missioners in Chile, provided clarification of Chile's political context. Terry Alexander, MM, and Madeline Dorsey, MM, shared the realities of living in 1980 El Salvador. Peter Hinde, O.Carm., and Margaret Swedish clarified the depiction of El Salvador history.

Carla's close friends, including Karen Crowe Schall-horn, Lillian Bozak DeLeo, Pat Cobb McKenny, and Karen Peterlin, shared their personal collections of her poems, letters, and art and also their often amusing stories of life with Carla. From the beginning of this project the Bill Ford family was gracious and generous. Bill made sure I had copies of Carla's poetry that his mother had copied from the archives years ago, as well as selected letters from Ita to her family.

Carla's sister, Betty, strongly encouraged this project; she was delighted that Carla's story would be shared. Betty supported the Maryknoll Sisters throughout her life; she remained in touch with Terry Alexander until she died in February 2009. I also met with several members of Carla's extended family in Wisconsin and benefited from the memories they shared. Rosemary Rupnow, Carla's cousin and godmother; Carol Ann "Tinkerbelle" Waltens, Betty's daughter; and Carla's cousin Mary Jo Thies have been especially supportive. David Meissner met with me to describe the two occasions he visited Carla in Chile when he was working as a journalist.

An unexpected privilege was the opportunity to travel in Carla's footsteps on trips to Chile and El Salvador sponsored by Maryknoll Lay Missioners "Friends Across Borders." In Chile I visited Pucón, Chillán, and Santiago's población La Bandera. There I met Miguel Cruz, a La Bandera resident who had worked with Carla, and Helen Carpenter, MM.

In 2005, the twenty-fifth anniversary of the churchwomen's deaths, I visited El Salvador. Our group traveled over mountain roads to Chalatenango, where Carla and Ita had worked, and visited their graves in the colorful cemetery. There I met Joan Uhlen, MM, who sat on a tombstone to lead hundreds in singing Carla and Ita's song "Lord of the Road." Pilgrims from America joined Chalatenango parishioners at the commemorative Mass where Carla was included in memorials to the four murdered churchwomen.

I am most grateful for the constant encouragement and support from the leadership of the Maryknoll Sisters. This book could not have been written without the resources contained in the Maryknoll Sisters Archives, and I am grateful for the guidance and assistance of Ellen Pierce, the director of the archives.

Last, but by no means least, I am deeply grateful for the services of my good friend Kathie Vint, who gave generously of her time and talent to assist me in this project. Kathie has been my right-hand mentor, wise critic, and first editor of my many rewrites. Her careful, intelligent contributions have greatly improved this work.

Notes

The Same Fate as the Poor collection in the Maryknoll Sisters Archives (MSA), Maryknoll, New York, provided major background material for this project. The collection, compiled by Judith Noone, contains letters and testimonies sent by family, friends, and colleagues of Carla after her death. It includes Carla's letters to her sister, Betty Frazier, her aunt Katherine Laudert, her mother's cousin Catherine Verbeten, OP, and to Becky Quinn, Ita Ford, Mrs. Mildred Ford, and fellow members of Maryknoll. The archives also contain Carla's letters to her closest spiritual advisors—George Ganss, SJ, Pedro Perez, OSB, and Cesar Jerez, SJ—as well as their written comments about her. Unless otherwise indicated, all direct quotes from Carla's letters, reflections, and reports; comments about her life that were submitted to the collection from 1980 to 1984; and the letters and other writings of Ita Ford are from *The Same Fate as the Poor* collection. Carla's poems are collected in *Carla's Creative Works*, Box 40 of the Maryknoll Sisters Archives.

The description of Sheila Cassidy's life, arrest, and detention in Chile is based on her 1982 book, *Audacity to Believe*. Material on the life of Archbishop Oscar Romero and 1977-1980 events in El Salvador is from *Romero: A Life* by James R. Brockman.

Chapter One

1. Mary Elizabeth Keyser, conversation with author, October 2005.

2. Betty Frazier, phone conversation with author, June 2005.

3. Mary Jo Thies, e-mail message to author, August 16, 2005.

Chapter Two

1. Noone, *Same Fate As the Poor*, 16.
2. Lernoux, *Hearts on Fire*, 129-130.
3. E-mail message to author, June 12, 2005.
4. Noone, 4.
5. E-mail message to author, June 17, 2006.
6. E-mail messages to author, October 25-26, 2005.
7. Ibid.
8. Ibid.
9. Ibid.
10. E-mail message to author, May 22, 2005.

Chapter Three

1. Noone, 4-5.
2. Cobb McKenny, phone conversation with author, June 2005.
3. Molineaux and Ress, *Maryknoll in Chile*, 423-436.
4. E-mail message to author, February 28, 2007.
5. Molineaux and Ress, 95.
6. E-mail message to author, February 28, 2007.
7. Molineaux and Ress, 89.
8. E-mail message to author, October 24, 2005.
9. Mary Lou Toiphal, conversation with author, October 2005.
10. E-mail messages to author, May 22-24, 2005.
11. E-mail message to author, May 9, 2005.
12. Molineaux and Ress, 162.
13. Lernoux, 166-176.
14. Molineaux and Ress, 163.
15. Phone conversation with author, January 2006.
16. U.S. Senate Staff Report, *Covert Action in Chile*. Senate investigators led by Sen. Frank Church documented covert U.S. spending of $3 million to influence the 1964 Chilean presidential elections and of $8 million more between 1970 and the 1973 coup. CIA director William Colby testified that the White House approved the covert actions.
17. Several of these resettlement areas, the poblaciones, surrounded Santiago. Each had its own name and community identity, but in all of them thousands of families—squatters and the jobless poor—occupied unused land and struggled to survive in harsh conditions.

18. Molineaux and Ress, 220.

19. Ibid, 232.

20. Molineaux and Ress, 242-243. An ecumenical group of missioners in Chile, many of them supporters of Christian socialism, published three open letters in defense of President Allende and Chile's democratic election of a socialist president. They sent the first letter to President Richard Nixon, the second to the president of ITT to protest his efforts against the confirmation of Allende as president, and the third, as a pastoral letter, to the leaders of Christian churches in the United States.

21. The description of Pat Cobb McKenny's deliberations during this period and her eventual decision to leave Maryknoll is based on her conversations, in person and on the phone, with the author, her e-mail messages to the author, and letters that Carla wrote her at the time.

22. David Meissner, conversation with author, March 6, 2007.

23. Phone conversation with author, February 26, 2006.

Chapter Four

1. Noone, 27.

2. E-mail message to author, March 9, 2006.

3. Phone conversation with author, January 2006.

4. Phone conversation with author, December 5, 2006.

5. Noone, 30.

6. Jara, 250-1.

7. Molineaux and Ress, 251; Flynn, e-mail message to author, February 21, 2006.

8. Molineaux and Ress, 274.

9. Ibid, 255.

10. Phone conversation with author, December 12, 2005.

11. Conversation with author, September 2006.

12. Noone, 35-36. A priest neighbor who taught courses in political science, including Marxism, at Catholic University, had buried the textbooks in his yard before his expulsion from Chile shortly after the coup. New residents, fearing reprisal if the authorities found the books, asked the sisters to keep them. "It was crazy," said Connie, "but they were perfectly good textbooks."

13. E-mail message to author, June 17, 2006.

14. Ford, *Here I Am, Lord*, 95-96.

15. Timerman, *Chile*, 69.

16. Phone conversation with author, December 12, 2005.

17. E-mail message to author, June 17, 2006.

18. E-mail message to author, March 9, 2006.

19. Phone conversation with author, July 16, 2006.

20. Noone, 35.

21. Conversation with author, October 2005.

22. Lernoux, xii.

23. Phone conversation with author, June 5, 2005.

24. Cassidy, *Audacity to Believe*, 114.

25. Today the site is Parque por la Paz. An inscription on a marker reads: "There was a time when death lay behind these walls but now, in this same place, there is life." An estimated 4,500 Chileans, including Michele Bachelet, president of Chile, were held at Villa Grimaldi.

26. Conversation with author, October 2006.

27. Cassidy, *Audacity*, 191-192.

28. Conversation with author, March 6, 2007.

Chapter Five

1. Carla's 1976 conversation with author; Frazier, phone conversation with author.

2. Phone conversation with author, April 17, 2007.

3. Benno Kornely, e-mail message to author, May 31, 2005.

4. E-mail message to author, May 31, 2005.

5. E-mail message to author.

6. Cassidy, phone conversation with author, June 5, 2005.

7. Cassidy, *Sharing the Darkness*, 116-117.

Chapter Six

1. Ford, 99-100. Since 1980, Ita's italicized words have inspired peace and justice advocates worldwide, particularly at events commemorating her and the other three churchwomen murdered in El Salvador.

2. Ibid, 101.

3. Ibid, 103-105.

4. Phone conversation with author, June 2005.

5. Noone, 42-43.

6. Ibid, 74.

7. Phone conversation with author, June 2005.

8. Noone, 74-76.

9. E-mail message to author, January 17, 2006.

10. The Puebla Documents were produced by the gathering of Latin American bishops in Puebla, Mexico, in early 1979. They reaffirmed their preferential option for the poor and their commitment to work for justice through grassroots-based church formation, known as Christian base communities.

11. Conversation with author, September 2006.

Chapter Seven

1. Joan Ratermann, conversations with author, October 2005 and May 2006.

2. Crowe Schallhorn, e-mail message to author.

3. Conversation with author, December 2005.

4. Lange and Iblacker, 144.

Chapter Eight

1. Nairn, Allan, "Behind the Death Squads," *The Progressive*, May 1984.

2. Archbishop Oscar Romero Biography, Kellogg Institute, University of Notre Dame, http://www.kellogg.nd.edu/Romero/pdfs.

3. Brockman, *Romero: A Life*, 20.

4. Costello, *Mission to Latin America*, 207.

5. Brockman, 131-132.

6. Carrigan, *Salvador Witness*, 95.

7. Carrigan, *Witness*, 108-110.

8. By the fall of that year the *Frente Farabundo Martí de Liberacion Nacional* was formed as the military defense of the rural peoples. The two groups later united as the FDR-FMLN.

9. Margaret Swedish, afterword to *The Same Fate As the Poor*, by Noone, 141-142. The United States sent advisors and more than $6 billion in military and security aid to El Salvador during the twelve-year civil war. U.S. fear of the spread of Communism had increased greatly after the Sandinista's successful revolution in Nicaragua in July 1979.

10. June Carolyn Erlick, "Last Chance for Peace," *National Catholic Reporter*.

11. Eric Green, "UN Condemns Both Sides," *USIA News Report*, March 17, 1993, http://www.fas.org/irp/news/1993/24847576-24851118.htm.

12. Brockman, 239.

13. In 1993 the UN Truth Commission reported that the as-

sassination had been ordered by Major Roberto D'Aubuisson, who the commission also cited for organizing death squads.

14. Noone, 97.

15. Maryknoll sisters in both Chile and El Salvador believe Carla composed the song while serving with them. Perhaps it took on greater meaning as Carla and Ita actually drove the difficult, hazardous roads in El Salvador. The words and music have since become familiar to many Maryknollers.

16. Ford, 169.

17. Hinde and Campbell, 22.

18. Noone, 104.

19. Ford, 172-174.

20. Noone, 101-102.

21. E-mail message and phone conversation with author, June 2005.

22. Hinde and Campbell, 11-12.

23. Carrigan, *Witness*, 175-176.

24. The petition sought international assistance to establish safety for refugees, hospital patients, and medical personnel. It was sent to several leaders in the United States, including Melinda Roper, MM, president of the Maryknoll Sisters; Annette Mulry, MM, administrator of the Maryknoll Sisters Office of Global Concerns; Archbishop John Quinn, president of the USCC; Tom Quigley, International Justice and Peace Office, USCC; and Dan Driscoll, Latin American Bureau, USCC.

25. On August 20, 1980, the State Department responded to Congressman Zablocki and Senator Gaylord Nelson's requests for information in a letter that claimed that my information was incorrect, that the International Red Cross did have representatives in El Salvador, and that the Salvadoran government was cooperating "consistent in its obligations under the Geneva Convention." It added, "El Salvador leftist guerilla groups are seeking international recognition of a state of civil war...and possible recognition as the legal Salvadoran government." After Carla's death, Zablocki pushed for further investigation by Secretary of State Edmund Muskie. A State Department reply on September 30, 1980, said: "The Salvadoran Government *recently* accepted an offer by the ICRC (International Red Cross) to provide assistance, support to detainees, services to families affected by terrorism, provision of general medical assistance." (Author's italics.)

26. Noone, 106.

27. Hinde, letter to author, June 27, 2009. Hinde and Campbell sent reports on their human rights findings to U.S. churches and solidarity groups in Washington, D.C. In 1981 they made a six-month speaking tour of the United States in order to correct disinformation the U.S. government was spreading about "their five martyred co-workers and dearest of friends." Hinde is also a co-founder of Christians for Peace in El Salvador (CRISPAZ), which has sent volunteers and delegations to El Salvador from 1984 to the present.

28. Carrigan, *Witness*, 192-193.

29. Hinde and Campbell, 12.

30. Carrigan, *Witness*, 197; Terry Alexander, e-mail message to author, January 29, 2009.

31. Hinde and Campbell, 11-12.

32. Phone conversation with author, July 16, 2006.

Bibliography

Benitez, Sandra. *Bitter Grounds.* New York: Hyperion, 1997.

————. *The Weight of All Things.* New York: Hyperion, 2000.

Berryman, Phillip. *The Religious Roots of Rebellion: Christians in Central American Revolutions.* Maryknoll, NY: Orbis Books, 1984.

Brett, Donna Whitson and Edward T. Brett. *Murdered in Central America: The Stories of Eleven U.S. Missionaries.* Maryknoll, NY: Orbis Books, 1988.

Brockman, James R. *Romero: A Life.* Maryknoll, NY: Orbis Books, 1989.

Carrigan, Ana. *Salvador Witness: The Life and Calling of Jean Donovan.* New York: Simon and Schuster, 1984.

Carrigan, Ana and Bernard Stone. *Roses in December,* videotape. New York: First Run Features, 1982.

Cassidy, Sheila. *Audacity to Believe.* Cleveland: Collins and World, 1978.

————. *Sharing the Darkness: The Spirituality of Caring.* Maryknoll, NY: Orbis Books, 1991.

Constable, Pamela and Arturo Valenzuela. *A Nation of Enemies: Chile under Pinochet.* New York: W.W. Norton, 1991.

Cooper, Marc. *Pinochet and Me: A Chilean Anti-Memoir.* London; New York: VERSO, 2001.

Costello, Gerald M. *Mission to Latin America: The Successes and Failures of a 20th Century Crusade.* Maryknoll, NY: Orbis Books, 1979.

Dear, John. *Jean Donovan: The Call to Discipleship.* Erie, PA: Pax Christi USA, 1987.

————. *Oscar Romero and the Nonviolent Struggle for Justice.* Erie, PA: Pax Christi USA, 2004.

Dickey, Christopher. "40 Killed in San Salvador." *Washington Post*, March 31, 1980.

Erlick, June Carolyn. "El Salvador: Last Chance for Peace." *National Catholic Reporter*, February 22, 1980.

————. "Slaughter in the Cathedral." *National Catholic Reporter*, April 11, 1980.

Ford, Ita. *Here I Am, Lord: The Letters and Writings of Ita Ford*. Edited by Jeanne Evans. Maryknoll, NY: Orbis Books, 2005.

Golden, Renny. *The House of the Poor, The House of Women: Salvadoran Women Spea*k. NY: Crossroad, 1991.

Green, Eric. *"UN Condemns Both Sides in Salvadoran Civil War."* United States Information Agency News Report, March 17, 1993.

Guzmán, Patricio. *The Battle of Chile*, videotape. New York: First Run/Icarus Films, 1976.

Hinde, Peter and Betty Campbell. *"Following the Star: The Liberation Process of the People of Cristo-Pueblo, El Salvador... of Archbishop Romero... of U.S. Women Martyrs."* A special issue of the newsletter of the Religious Task Force. Washington, DC, 1981.

Jara, Joan. *An Unfinished Song: The Life of Victor Jara*. New York: Ticknor and Fields, 1984.

Kazel, Dorothy Chapon. *Alleluia Woman: Sister Dorothy Kazel, OSU*. Cleveland: Chapel Publications, 1987.

Lange, Martin and Reinhold Iblacker, editors. *Witnesses of Hope: The Persecution of Christians in Latin Americ*a. Maryknoll, NY: Orbis Books, 1981.

Lernoux, Penny. With Arthur Jones and Robert Ellsberg. *Hearts on Fire: The Story of the Maryknoll Sisters*. Maryknoll, NY: Orbis Books, 1993.

Molineaux, David J. and Mary Judith Ress. *Maryknoll in Chile: The First 50 Years*. Chile: Mosquito Editores, 1993.

Nairn, Allan. "Behind the Death Squads." *The Progressive*, May 1984.

Noone, Judith M. *The Same Fate as the Poor*, rev. ed. Maryknoll, NY: Orbis Books, 1995.

Russell, Stephanie. "Millions Mourn Slain Romero." *National Catholic Reporter*, April 4, 1980.

Swedish, Margaret and Marie Dennis. *Like Grains of Wheat: A Spirituality of Solidarity*. Maryknoll, NY: Orbis Books, 2004.

Timerman, Jacobo. *Chile: Death in the South.* New York: Knopf, 1987.

UN Truth Commission. Report of the Commission on the Truth for El Salvador. *From Madness to Hope: The 12 Year War in El Salvador.* New York: March 1993.

U.S. Senate Staff Report to Select Committee to Study Governmental Operations with Respect to Intelligence Activities. *Covert Action in Chile, 1963-1973.* Washington, DC: U.S. Government Printing Office, 1975.

Zagano, Phyllis. *Ita Ford: Missionary Martyr.* New York: Paulist Press, 1996.